THE FOLKSINGER'S GUITAR GUIDE

An Instruction Manual by Jerry Silverman

Based on the Folkways Record by Pete Seeger

N OAK PUBLICATION, n.y.

Original Illustrations: Jim Infantino
Prints, Engravings and Photos
    selected and arranged by   Moses Asch
Layout and additional illustrations: Ethel Raim

Twenty Second Printing   April, 1973

Music Sales Limited
78 Newman Street, London W. 1

Printed in the United States of America
ISBN No. 0-8256-0013-8

CONTENTS

INTRODUCTION

This is not a "compleat" method for the folk guitar.

It is doubtful whether such a book could be written for there are as many individual styles of playing folk guitar as there are individual folks who play folk guitar. Each person could write his own book.

Some people have done so already.

What we have attempted here is to set forth some basic principles of <u>North American</u>* folk guitar styles not so much from the point of view of how many chords and songs you can play by the end of the first...second... third...fourth week...but rather, what to do with those chords and songs after you have learned them.

Many people who study or play folk guitar honestly feel that learning chords is the be-all and end-all of the folk guitar. How many times have you heard the expression: "I just want to be able to chord along.."?

Well, the "chord" part is easy but what do you do with the "along"?

In other words, merely "chording along" is very far from the whole story. It is in the imaginative use of folk rhythms and strums that real beauty can be achieved with the guitar.

In the quest of "beauty" you will find very soon that folk music must become a way of life, not merely a study. This book - any book - even a teacher can only hope to point you in the right direction and give you a gentle push. The rest of the journey is up to you. The road may be a bit bumpy at first but you may take comfort in this:

You are not travelling the road alone.

Get acquainted**with those who have travelled it before...

Leadbelly	Elizabeth Cotton
Blind Lemon Jefferson	Merle Travis
Big Bill Broonzy	Fred Gerlach
Jimmy Rodgers	Lightning Hopkins
Woody Guthrie	The Carter Family
Brownie McGhee	Erik Darling
Chet Atkins	Furry Lewis
Odetta	Joan Baez
Richard Dyer-Bennet	Lonnie Johnson
Josh White	Frank Hamilton
Tom Paley	Cisco Houston
Jack Elliott	Rev. Gary Davis

AND MANY MORE!

...And also find out who is travelling along side with you. If you live in a big city chances are there is already an active folkmusical life. In smaller communities you may be able to whip up enthusiasm (if it isn't there already) by posting the following notice in your library, Y, community center...

WANTED * WANTED * WANTED *

interested folks who sing folksongs and who play guitar and banjo (etc.) to get together every now and then to play guitar and banjo (etc.) please contact . . .

I know of one incident where someone hung up a sign in his local library and before he could turn around the librarian had joined the group.

AS FAR AS THIS BOOK IS CONCERNED,

please remember that the examples illustrated in the following pages are just that: examples. As you practice your new techniques on the songs given here you should also begin to apply them to the many, many songs to be found in many, many other collections (see page 79) and as you gain confidence and skill you will be able to pick up songs from records and live performances. "Live performances" by the way, is a key expression in this general discussion of approaches to the folk guitar. To get to know how things really are done you must actually observe the player in action. Since there are so many individual styles one never stops learning if one can get to see as well as hear as many guitarists as possible.

---

* We blush when we think of all the complex and beautiful South American rhythms which we have not gone into in this book. When we say "folk" we self consciously mean north of the Rio Grande and south of the Distant Early Warning Line except for one brief glance at the West Indies.

** See list of recordings on P. 78

For what may be the finest word on the subject of how to approach your study of the folk guitar let's call upon Woody Guthrie:

I can't play any chord by looking at any book and never could,...I'll bet you the chording books that Leadbelly has used in his greening and grey years wouldn't make a pile big enough for you to find on your floor. Leadbelly learnt to play the guitar the same way I did, by "ear", by "touch" by "feel", by "bluff", by "gessin", by "fakin" and by a great crave and drive to keep on playing.

I learned that I could plunk along on "Birmingham Jail" in the key of, say, G and get by plumb fine and dandy with only one chord change in the whole song, up to D and back to greasy G. A few Chicago boilermakers has caused me to get real flirty at labor union lawn parties and toss in a C somewheres along there where you're down on your knees.

If I'm sort of lazing it around, I leave out a few of the extrays. If I'm scattering wild oats for my goats, I lay in a few more just to keep my string finger oily and limber. If I play with one other instrument, I do it this way. If it's two others, I play some other way. If it's at a sixteen guitar hoot, I am forced by all of the laws of nature and averages to naturally find some 17th lost part nobody else is using and

tickle away with that. I never do play the same song twice alike.

I've pounded out "Ida Red", "Old Judge Parker Take Your Shackles Offa Me" for as high as thirty or forty minutes with no more than two chords D to A, D to A, and D to A ten blue jillion times through a square dance. Lots of the old fullblodded fiddlers will toss you down off from his platform if you go to getting too fancy with your chording.

I'm high in favor of books and chord books, pictures, drawings, illustrations and so forth and so on. But don't let them get tangled up in your throw rope. Don't let them worry you, nor slow you down, nor stop you. Use your eyes, watch other good, bad and medium players, do like they do. Learn a wiggle from one, a slide from the next, a tickle from the next one, a whang and bang, a walkalong from somebody else, and before you know it, you'll be just as good a doubler and faker, lead finger, and follower, as the rest of them.

Woody Guthrie
Coney Islands on the Lowlands by the Foamings of the Se

AMEN !

HOW TO HOLD THE GUITAR

The two most commonly used types of guitar for folksong accompaniment.
See page 74 for a discussion of the relative merits of these instruments.

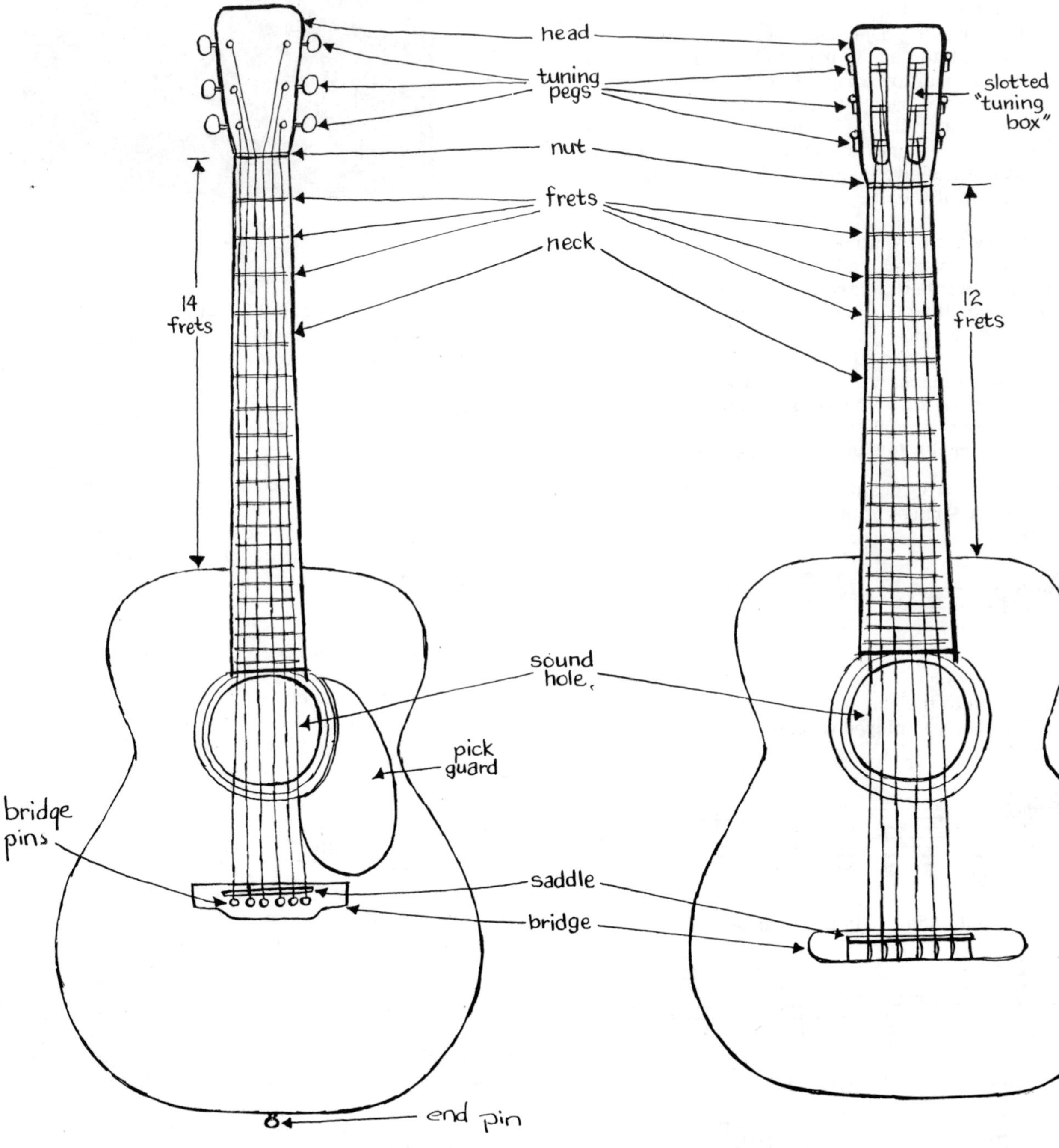

head

tuning
pegs

slotted
"tuning
box"

nut

frets

neck

14
frets

12
frets

sound
hole

pick
guard

bridge
pins

saddle

bridge

end pin

"FLAT TOP STEEL-STRING"

"CLASSICAL NYLON-STRING"

TABLATURE

Ever since the invention of music notation countless generations of instrumentalists have been trying to avoid learning to read music. During the last 700 years or so elaborate systems have been developed to show the player which holes to cover, which key to press, which string to pluck or which fret to stop, instead of the actual note on the musical staff.

The general desire to avoid learning to read music is nowhere more prevalent than among "folk" instrumentalists and singers. They consider - perhaps, rightly so - the printed music page to be an intrusion upon a highly personal art form. A form whose greatest practitioners have not been fettered by pieces of paper. A form where creation and performance often took place in the same breath - a breath that was often labored due to the swinging of a sledge hammer, the pulling of a rope or the lifting of a bale.

If in the very act of writing such a book as this we do violence to this sacred tradition it is only in an effort to preserve it. But then we are squarely faced with a circular paradox: How can you teach music without, in fact, teaching music?

A three-fold compromise was indicated: Combine standard music notation with guitar tablature and continually try to impress upon the student the necessity of listening to as much folk guitar playing as possible.

In guitar tablature it is customary to use six lines to represent the six strings of the instrument, as follows:

The numbers above each line indicate at what fret the string is pressed to the fingerboard by a finger of the left hand. Thus, if you played a scale starting on the lowest string

tablature would show it in this manner:

chords would be given thus:

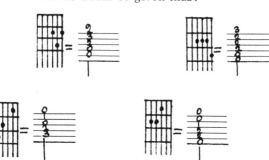

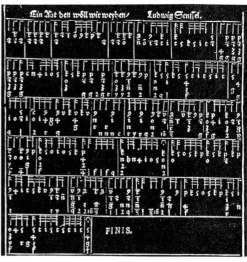

Time values are indicated by small stems below the bottom line of the diagram in accordance with standard musical notation as follows:

Between the tablature and the music notation itself will appear symbols to indicate which fingers of the right hand pluck which strings.

Thus: T = thumb
      I = index finger
      M = middle finger
      R = ring finger
      L = little finger
      H = "hammering on" (see p. 34)

TUNING THE GUITAR

The customary first step in the study of a stringed instrument is to teach the student how to tune it. While this may seem like the obvious beginning there are a number of difficulties to be overcome.

A sense of pitch - the ability to determine the relative "highness" and "lowness" - of notes, while indispensable to a musician, may not be present in its most sensitive, refined degree at the beginning of study.

The determination of whether one string is higher or lower than "it should be" is a highly sophisticated process. And even if that determination has been made "what to do about it" may cause further problems.

When you start comparing notes on the guitar to supposedly corresponding notes on the piano or the pitch pipe you have to be able to discount the obvious (and sometimes confusing) difference in tonal quality - timbre - (a piano doesn't really sound like a guitar) - to distinguish tonal quality from pitch variation.

It is the rare, fortunate beginner who is able to "hear his way through" all this and come up with an in-tune instrument.

However, a sense of pitch can be developed, trained and refined in most people so that "after a while" (a necessarily vague expression) guitars do get tuned.

Therefore, the following information on tuning is presented here more for reference - present and future - than to be mastered before any further progress is made on the guitar.

If the string you are tuning is too low in comparison with the piano you must tighten it to raise the pitch, if it is too high it must be loosened. As you turn the tuning gear remember to keep playing the string to hear which way it is going and to know when to stop.

Notice that the interval between the 6th and 5th strings (E f g A) is four notes. More precisely, it is called a "perfect fourth". A to D is also a perfect fourth - likewise D to G. The next pair of strings are a "major third" apart (G a B) and the last two (B-E) are a perfect fourth again.

A Pitchpipe - is a little whistle or set of whistles tuned to one - or all six - of the strings of the guitar. A common 6 note pitch pipe looks like this:

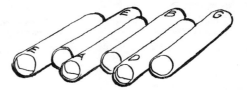

The one great advantage of a pitch pipe over a piano is that it fits into your guitar case easier than a piano.

The internal relationship between the strings - or "relative pitch" - leads us to another way of tuning commonly used when no standard pitch (like a piano or pitchpipe) is present.

1) Assume your lowest string is fairly on pitch.

2) Press that string down just below the 5th fret.

   The 5th string, next to it, should now sound the same pitch.

3) Now press the 5th string down at the 5th fret.

   The 4th string should now sound this pitch.

4) Press the 4th string down at the same place, and the third string should sound the same pitch.

5) Press the third string down just below the 4th fret, and it should sound the same as the 2nd string.

6) Press the 2nd string down just below the 5th fret again, and tune the 1st string to it. The 1st string should now be just exactly two octaves above the 6th string.

As you become more experienced your initial assumption as to the correctness of the pitch of the 6th string will be less fanciful. A good guitar player may not have "perfect pitch" (a gift of the Gods) but he will be able to tell pretty accurately if his starting point is anywhere near the mark.

The final stage in tuning by relative pitch is achieved when one can play, say, the 6th string and hear "in advance" what the others should sound like.

That may take a while...

CHORD DIAGRAMS AND CHORDS

For the notation of chords we shall use the standard "chord diagram" as well as the musical notation and the tablature for each chord. The diagram is an "aerial view" of the fingerboard of the guitar.

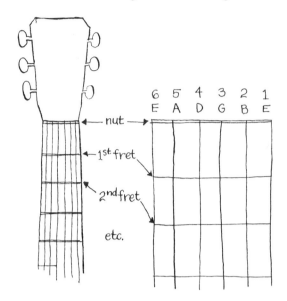

Now we will learn our first two chords.

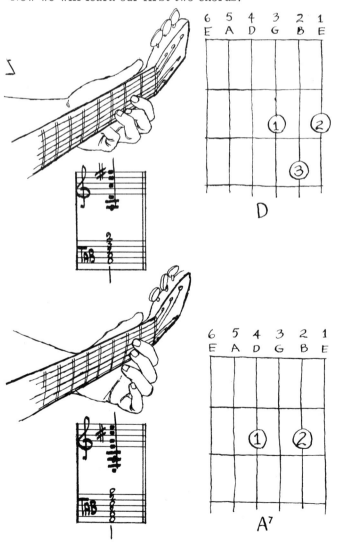

The numbers in the circles represent the fingers of the left hand. Make sure that the fingernails of this hand are trimmed as closely as possible. You have to press almost straight down on the strings to avoid accidentally touching more than one string at a time. Long fingernails would make this finger position difficult if not impossible.

Place the fingers of the left hand as close to the higher numbered fret (as shown in the diagram) as possible without actually touching the fret. Press down hard. The object is to bring the strings firmly into contact with the proper frets.

Your fingertips may become sore from pressing down the strings. The best thing to do in the beginning is to practice for short periods of time - but often. After a week or so the tenderness will disappear (if the fingers haven't done so first).

NOTE how easy it is to change from D to A7 and from A7 to D. The first and second fingers move as a unit (more or less) from strings three and one (for D) to four and two (for A7) The third finger just pops up and down at the right time...Easy?

You can play dozens of songs using the D and A7 chords (and quite a few with just D alone).

Try some of these songs using just D to get the feel of playing and singing at the same time. Use the thumb of your right hand to strum over all the strings in a downward direction.

WARNING: Do not play on each syllable of every word. Rather start strumming with a slow, steady, evenly pulsed beat and sing the words "rhythmically" over the accompaniment.

> Row, row, row your boat
> Gently down the stream.
> Merrily, merrily, merrily, merrily,
> Life is but a dream.

Frere Jacques, Frere Jacques,
Dormez vous, dormez vous?
Sonnez les matines, sonnez les matines.
Dan, dan, don. Dan, dan, don.

> Swing low, sweet chariot
> Coming for to carry me home
> Swing low, sweet chariot
> Coming for to carry me home

> I looked over Jordan, and what did I see
> Coming for to carry me home
> A band of angels coming after me
> Coming for to carry me home

> Swing low, etc.

RIGHT HAND: Let your nails grow somewhat longer on your right hand. You'll need them a little later for some of the strums we're going to learn.

Froggy went a-courtin and he did ride, uh huh
Froggy went a-courtin and he did ride
Sword and pistol by his side, uh huh

(3426 ½ more verses)

Oh, you take the high road,
And I'll take the low road,
And I'll be in Scotland before you.
For me and my true love will never
     meet again
By the bonny, bonny banks of Loch
     Lomond.

I am a roving gambler, I've gambled all around
Whenever I meed with a deck of cards, I lay my
     money down.

I've gambled down in Washington, I've gambled over
     in Spain
I'm on my way to Georgia to lay down my last game.

I had not been in Washington many more weeks than
     three
When I fell in love with a pretty little girl, and she
     fell in love with me.

She took me to her parlor, she cooled me with her
     fan
She whispered low in her mother's ear, I love that
     gambling man.

Oh daughter, dearest daughter, how could you treat
     me so
To leave your poor old mother and with a gambler go.

Oh mother, dearest mother, you know I love you well
But the love I hold for the gambling man no human
     tongue can tell.

I wouldn't marry a farmer, he's always in the rain
The man I want's the gambling man, he wears that
     big gold chain.

I wouldn't marry a doctor, he's always gone from
     home
The man I want's the gambling man, he won't leave
     me alone.

I hear the train a coming, she's coming round the
     curve
She's whistling and a blowing and straining every
     nerve.

Oh mother, dearest mother, I'll tell you if I can
If you ever see me coming back, it'll be with the
     gambling man.

* * * * * * * * * * * * * * * * * * *

Later on you will see that it is possible to enrich
the sound of these songs by adding other chords to them.

BASS - CHORD THUMB STRUM

Now take the D chord and just pluck the fourth string
with the thumb of your right hand. Then brush down
across the rest (3rd, 2nd, 1st) of the strings.

Now try the same thing with the A7 chord. Only this
time pluck the fifth string with your thumb and brush
down over the first four strings.

Try it over and over until it comes easy...

When you can do that so well that you don't need to
think about it, you're the man with an educated thumb...
Or the girl with the educated thumb.....

Now we're ready to try some songs with the D and
A7 chords played in this "oom-pah" manner.

> Always start strumming the first chord before you
> start singing. This "introduction" will give you the
> pitch of the first note and help get you "in the mood".

SKIP TO MY LOU

SKIP, SKIP   SKIP TO MY LOU

THIS SYMBOL MEANS "REPEAT THE PRECEEDING MEASURE"

SKIP, SKIP   SKIP TO MY LOU

SKIP, SKIP   SKIP TO MY LOU

SKIP TO MY LOU MY   DAR - LING

That was the chorus - here are the verses - sung and played the same way.

Lost my partner, what'll I do
A7
Lost my partner what'll I do.
D
Lost my partner, what'll I do.
A7   D
Skip to my lou my darling.

I'll get another one prettier than you...
Flies in the buttermilk, shoo, fly, shoo...
Little red wagon painted blue...
Gone again, skip to my lou...

* * * * * * * * * * * * * * * * * * *

Get used to the idea of hearing when and where the chords change. Don't think of the chords as changing on a particular word - rather, listen to what is going on in the melody when a chord change is indicated. Then try playing another verse and hear if you can spot the same place in the melody where the chord changed in the first verse.

THE OLD CHISHOLM TRAIL

WELL, COME A - LONG BOYS AND

LIS-TEN TO MY TALE AND I'LL TELL YOU OF MY TROU-BLES ON THE

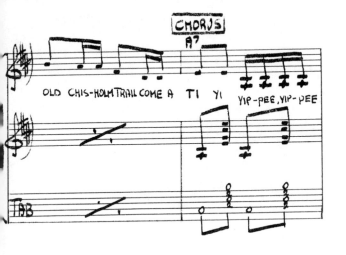

I started up the trail October 23rd,
I started up the trail with the 2-U herd...

I jumped in the saddle and grabbed a-holt the horn,
Best durn cowboy ever was born...

I'm up in the morning before daylight
And before I sleep, the moon shines bright...

It's bacon and beans 'most every day,
I'd as soon been a-eating prairie hay...

Cloudy in the east and it looks like rain,
And my damned old slicker's in the wagon again...

Wind began to blow - rain began to fall,
It looked, by grab, like we was gonna loose 'em all...

A heifer went loco and the boss said, "Kill it".
I shot it in the arse with the handle of a skillet...

I went to the boss to draw my roll,
He had me figgered out nine dollars in the hole...

So me and the boss, we had a little chat,
I hit him in the face with my big slouch hat...

So the boss said to me, "I'm gonna fire you -
"And not only you but the whole damn crew"...

Well, I'm going back home to draw my money,
Going back home to see my honey...

On a ten-dollar hoss and a forty-dollar saddle,
I'm a-going to punch them Texas cattle...

Well, My feet are in the stirrup and my saddle's in the sky,
And I'll quit punching cows in the Sweet Bye and Bye...

* * * * * * * * * * * * * * * * * * * *

Chords are generally played in standard combinations with other chords. These combinations comprise what are known musically as "keys". We have been playing in the key of D (major). If we learn one other chord in the key of D we will literally be able to play thousands of songs.

The third chord we need to know in the key of D is G.

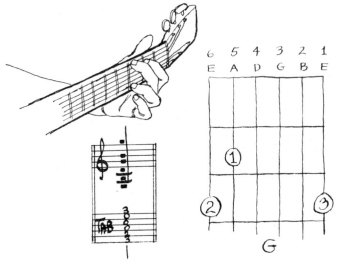

The thumb of the right hand strikes the 6th string and strums over the rest of the strings as with D and A7.

Play back and forth with these three chords until you know them so well that you can sing a song without thinking about them.

ATTENTION FINGERNAIL BITERS...

If you really must, then please direct your efforts to your left hand only...

13

WORRIED MAN BLUES

I went across the river, and I lay down to sleep
  (3 times)
When I woke up, had shackles on my feet.

Twenty nine links of chain around my leg (3 times)
And on each link, an initial of my name.

I asked that judge, tell me, what's gonna be my fine?
  (3 times)
Twenty one years on the Rocky Mountain Line.

Twenty one years to pay my awful crime (3 times)
Twenty one years - but I got ninety-nine.

The train arrived twenty one coaches long (3 times)
The girl I love is on that train and gone.

I looked down the track as far as I could see (3 times)
Little bitty hand was waving after me.

If anyone should ask you, who composed this song
  (3 times)
Tell him was I, and I sing it all day long.

* * * * * * * * * * * * * * * * * * *

14

SAINTS

And when the sun refuse to shine...
And when the moon drips red with blood...
And when the revelation comes...
And when the new world is revealed...

By this time you may have noticed that you were not able comfortably to sing all the songs we have introduced so far. Skip To My Lou may have been too high or Worried Man may have been too low.

If this is the case (or similarly with any of the other songs) don't worry - there is nothing wrong with you. Not all people sing the same songs in the same keys. In fact the same song may be sung and played (depending on the individual vocal range of the performer) in any one of twelve keys. To begin to accomodate to various situations we obviously need to know some more chords and also how to transpose (that is, to change) from one key to another.

KEY OF A MAJOR

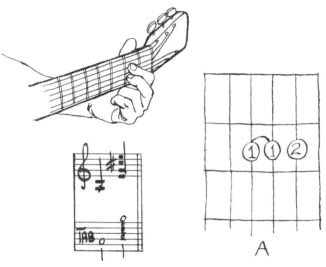

Thumb plucks the A string.

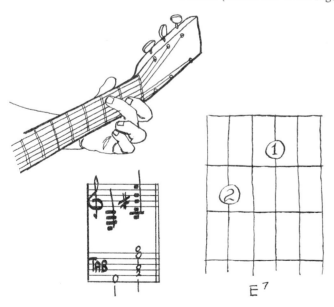

Thumb plucks the E string.

The third chord in the key of A is D, which you already know.

TRANSPOSING

Now you are ready to transpose some of your songs if necessary as well as learn lots of new ones.

If we visualize the notes of a key as an alphabetical series ("scale") for the key of D we get the following:

1	2	3	4	5	6	7
D	E	F#	G	A	B	C#

(Don't worry about the sharps now)

The key of A gives us this:

1	2	3	4	5	6	7
A	B	C#	D	E	F#	G#

Notice that in the key of D - D, G and A are the first, fourth and fifth notes of the scale and that these three notes correspond in position to A, D and E in the key of A.

Likewise the D, G, A7 chords correspond to the A, D, E7. Try playing some of the songs you have already had with these new chords and see what happens.

And remember those numbers I, IV, V which represent the relationship between the three main chords in any key. You'll be using those numbers time and again to help you transpose many songs from key to key. The I, IV and V chords are called the "Tonic", "Subdominant" and "Dominant", respectively.

BASIC RIGHT-HAND FINGER STRUM

Before going on with the learning of new chords let's try something new with the right hand. Instead of just brushing your thumb down across the top three strings we will now employ the fingers of the right hand in plucking those strings. The thumb will now strike only the bass string of the chord. Place your fingers on the first three strings as follows:

Index finger on the third string
Middle finger on the second string
Ring finger on the first string

The thumb rests on either the E, A or D string depending on the chord. Keep the wrist somewhat arched and the thumb at right angles to the direction of movement of the fingers. (Sort of an inverted hitch-hiker's position.)

EXERSIZE: (sic.)

1. With the fingers resting lightly on the proper strings strike the 6th string several times with the thumb. Do not move the fingers while moving the thumb.
2. With the thumb resting on the 6th string pluck the three strings gently by moving the fingers upward and inward as if clenching a fist (but not all the way - just enough to sound the strings). **DON'T MOVE YOUR WRIST.**
3. Now alternate first the thumb then the fingers.
4. Play a few chords and see what it sounds like. That muffled sound you hear is probably a result of the fingers of your left hand not pressing down properly.
5. Be careful **NOT TO BEND YOUR THUMB** as you pluck the bass notes. Particularly important when playing a D chord; otherwise your thumb moving down will "bump into" your fingers moving up.

JOHN BROWN'S BODY

JOHN BROWN'S BO-DY LIES A—MOULD-RING IN THE GRAVE

JOHN BROWN'S BO-DY LIES A—MOULD-RING IN THE GRAVE

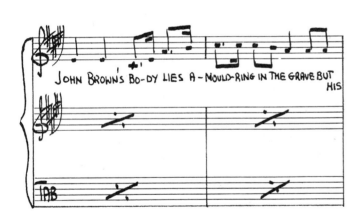

JOHN BROWN'S BO-DY LIES A—MOULD-RING IN THE GRAVE BUT HIS

SOUL GOES MARCH-ING ON

Chorus (same chords as the verse)
Glory, glory hallelujah (3 times)
But his soul goes marching on.

John Brown died that the slave might be free (3 times)
And his soul goes marching on.

He captured Harper's Ferry with his nineteen men, so
      true,
And he frightened Old Virginia till she trembled through
      and through,
They hung him for a traitor - they themselves the traito[r]
      crew,
But his soul goes marching on.

The stars in heaven are looking kindly down (3 times)
On the grave of old John Brown.

Now has come the glorious jubilee (3 times)
When all mankind is free.

* * * * * * * * * * * * * * * * * * * *

Let's take a closer look at the LEFT HAND. Are
all the notes of the chords sounding clearly. You think
so? How about the first string when you play A. This
should be an open (unfingered) string. If you grip the
neck of the guitar too tightly you may muffle one or
more of the strings. Lower your left wrist so that your
palm does not come completely in contact with the neck.
And curve those fingers around so that they can approac[h]
the strings in a nearly vertical manner.

Don't confuse the neck of your guitar with a baseball
bat or tennis racket.

THREE-QUARTER ($\frac{3}{4}$) TIME

The songs that we have had up to now are in what is called duple meter (or duple time). That is the basic rhythmic feeling is either "one-two one-two", or "one-two-three-four". [$\frac{2}{4}$ or $\frac{4}{4}$] On the guitar, as you know these are played in an "oom-pah" alternation of bass-note and chord. Many songs, however are in triple meter or most commonly three-quarter time ($\frac{3}{4}$). Note: these time signatures are not fractions. It is not three divided by four but an indication that there are three (or two, or four) quarter notes in each measure. $\frac{3}{4}$ time is often referred to as "waltz time."

To play in $\frac{3}{4}$ time the most common practise is as follows:

First beat: THUMB plucks bass note
Second beat: FINGERS pluck up
Third beat: FINGERS pluck up

Count: 1 - 2 - 3 1 - 2 - 3 1 - 2 - 3

Hear the wind blow, love, hear the wind blow,
Hang your head over, hear the wind blow.

If you don't love me, love whom you please.
Throw your arms 'round me give my heart ease.

Give my heart ease love, give my heart ease,
Throw your arms 'round me give my heart ease.

Write me a letter send it by mail,
Send it in care of the Birmingham Jail.

Birmingham Jail, love, Birmingham Jail,
Send it in care of the Birmingham Jail.

Build me a castle forty feet high,
So I can see her as she rides by.

As she rides by, love, as she rides by,
So I can see her as she rides by.

Roses love sunshine, violets love dew,
Angels in heaven know I love you.

Know I love you dear, know I love you,
Angels in heaven know I love you.

* * * * * * * * * * * * * * * * * * *

DARK AS A DUNGEON

by Merle Travis

IT'S DARK AS A DUN-GEON WAY

DOWN IN THE MINES

Now it's many a man I have seen in my day
Who has lived just to labor his whole life away.
Like a fiend with his dope and a drunkard his wine,
A man will have lust for the lure of the mine.(Cho.)

I hope when I die and the ages shall roll
My body will blacken and turn into coal.
Then I'll look from the door of my heavenly home,
And pity the miners a digging my bones. (Cho.)

* * * * * * * * * * * * * * * * * * * *

What Next?

Learning chords on the guitar is pretty much of a routine matter. You can look at the chord chart in the back of this book and get many chords as you need them. What is important is: What to do with chords once you have learned them. We need to learn methods of strumming and other variations that will make your folk accompaniments (and instrumental solos - eventually) more interesting.

ALTERNATING BASS

The first step is to realize that your thumb may strike other strings in each chord beside the basic bass note. Your thumb may <u>alternate</u> from string to string as follows:

D Chord: Alternate between D string and A string.

A and A7: Alternate between A string and E and/or D string.

G: Alternate between E string and A and/or D string.

E7: Alternate between E string and A and/or D string.

For all other chords the alternate bass strings will be indicated in the diagrams.

In $\frac{3}{4}$ time the alternation proceeds similarly. Just remember - two upstrokes for each downstroke.

21

BASS RUNS

An endless series of "oom-pahs" - bass-chord, bass-chord, bass-chord... can soon get monotonous. In an effort to introduce more variety into your playing we now turn to a consideration of "bass runs". A bass run as the name implies, is a series of single notes played on the bass strings. These runs are usually played as a substitute for the last two or three beats of a chord just prior to the arrival of a new chord. In some cases they may themselves sound like a melody.

The actual series of notes which comprises a bass run is generally made up of the notes of the scale connecting the roots of the two chords involved. The following examples will illustrate:

A - E₇ (E) - A

D - A (A7) - D

A (or A⁷)

D

D - G - D

A - E₇ (E) - A

23

Here's a song in which all these runs can be played.

UNION MAID
by Woody Guthrie

It is not necessary to play all the possible runs
every time. Moderation in everything...

2. This Union Maid was wise, to the tricks of Company
   spies
   She couldn't be fooled by company stools, she'd always
   organize the guys.
   She'd always get her way when she struck for higher pay,
   She'd show her card to the company guard and this is
   what she'd say: (Cho.)

3. Now you gals who want to be free, just take this tip from
   me,
   Get you a man who's a union man and join the Ladies
   Auxilliary.
   Married life ain't hard when you've got a union card,
   And a union man has a happy life when he's got a union
   wife. (Cho.)

Bass runs can be played in all keys. We need to learn three more "primary" keys (C, G and E) to complete our basic chord vocabulary. In the following songs we will introduce the new chords and the new runs together. It is not necessary for you to play the runs until the chords have been mastered - they are presented here for reference purposes.

THE KEY OF G MAJOR

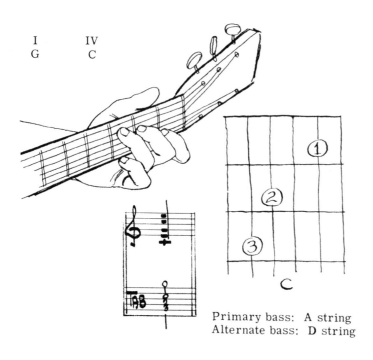

I   IV
G   C

Primary bass: A string
Alternate bass: D string

V7
D7

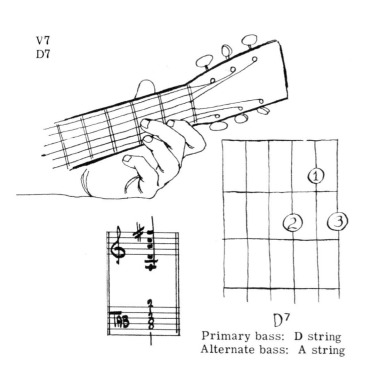

Primary bass: D string
Alternate bass: A string

JESSE JAMES

JES-SE JAMES WAS A LAD WHO

KILLED MAN-Y A MAN HE ROBBED THE GLEN-DALE

TRAIN HE STOLE FROM THE RICH AND

GAVE TO THE POOR HE'D A HAND AND A HEART AND A

26

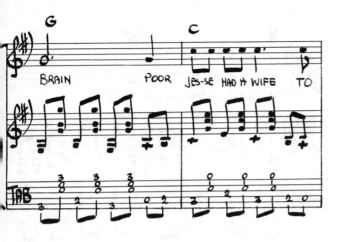

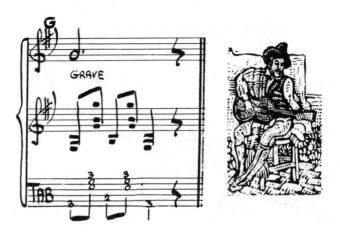

It was Robert Ford that dirty little coward,
I wonder how he does feel
For he ate of Jesse's bread and he slept in Jesse's bed,
And he laid poor Jesse in his grave.

How the people held their breath when they heard of
    Jesse's death
And wondered how he ever came to die.
It was one of the gang called Little Robert Ford
That shot poor Jesse on the sly.

Jesse was a man a friend to the poor,
He never would see a man suffer pain.
And with his brother Frank he robbed the Chicago bank,
And stopped the Glendale train.

It was on a Wednesday night the moon was shining bright,
They stopped the Glendale train.
And the people they did say for many miles away,
It was robbed by Frank and Jesse James.

They went to a crossing not very far from there,
And there they did the same.
With the agent on his knees, he delivered up the keys
To the outlaws Frank and Jesse James.

It was on a Saturday night Jesse was at home,
Talking to his family brave.
Robert Ford came along like a thief in the night
And laid poor Jesse in his grave.

This song was made by Billy Gashade
As soon as the news did arrive.
He said there was no man with the law in his hand
Who could take Jesse James while alive.

* * * * * * * * * * * * * * * * * *

THE KEY OF E MAJOR

I
E

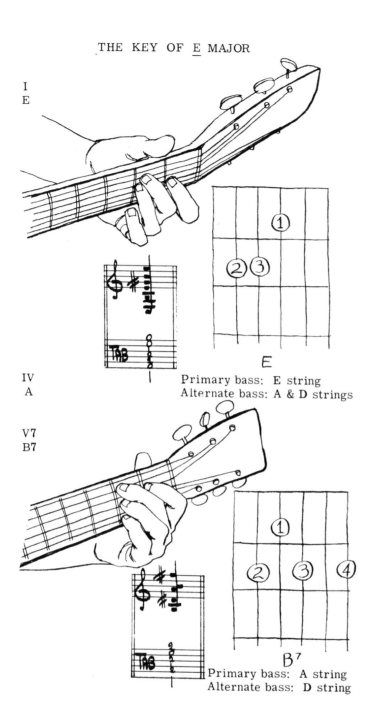

E

Primary bass: E string
Alternate bass: A & D strings

IV
A

V7
B7

B⁷

Primary bass: A string
Alternate bass: D string

'NEATH THE WEEP-ING WIL-LOW TREE

WHEN HE HEARS HIS LOVE IS SLEEP-ING

MAY - BE THEN HE'LL THINK OF ME

BURY ME BENEATH THE WILLOW

BU - RY ME BE - NEATH THE WIL-LOW

My heart is sad and I am lonely
Thinking of one I love
When will I meet him? Oh, no never,
Unless we meet in heaven above.

Tomorrow was to be our wedding,
I pray, Oh Lord, where can he be.
He's gone he's gone to love some other;
He no longer cares for me.

He told me that he dearly loved me,
How could I believe him untrue.
Until one day some neighbors told me,
He has proven untrue to you.

* * * * * * * * * * * * * * * * * * *

28

THE KEY OF C MAJOR

I   IV
C   F

V7
G7

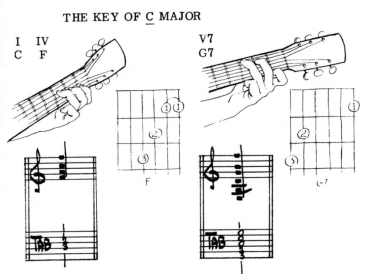

Primary bass: D string
Alternate bass: A string

Primary bass: E string
Alternate bass: A & D string

The F chord may present some problems because of the manner in which the first finger must cover two strings at once. To get it to sound properly you must keep your wrist arched and the first finger as straight as possible.

HARD AIN'T IT HARD

CHORUS   C

IT'S   HARD AND IT'S HARD, AIN'T IT

F   C

HARD   TO LOVE ONE WHO NE-VER DOES LOVE

G7   C

YOU   IT'S HARD AND IT'S HARD, AIN'T IT

F   C   G7

HARD GREAT GOD TO LOVE ONE WHO NE-VER WILL BE

C

TRUE

There is a place in this old town,
And that's where my true love lays around.
And he takes other women down on his knee,
For to tell them what he never does tell me.

Don't go there a drinking and a gambling,
Don't go there your sorrows for to drown.
That hard likker place is a low-down disgrace,
It's the meanest damn' place in this town.

The first time I saw my true love,
He was standing in the door.
And the last time I saw his false-hearted face,
He was dead on the barroom floor.

* * * * * * * * * * * * * * * * * * * *

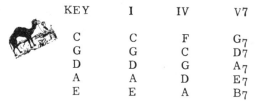

We have learned to date, these chords in the following keys:

KEY	I	IV	V7
C	C	F	G_7
G	G	C	D_7
D	D	G	A_7
A	A	D	E_7
E	E	A	B_7

These are the five basic major keys of the folk guitar. With them you can play and sing literally thousands of American and other folk songs.

If any of the preceding songs is in a key which is either too high or too low for your voice you should transpose it to a more comfortable singing key.

Bass runs in $\frac{3}{4}$ time will be incorporated into the next lesson.

THE RIGHT HAND

Now that you are familiar with most of the basic chords and have some facility in playing runs we will turn our attention to what should be the most interesting facet of folk guitar playing: Rhythm - that is, right-hand techniques.

Arpeggios: This is one of the many words in the lexicon of music which is borrowed from the Italian. It comes from the word arpa - harp. You all know how a harp sounds when its strings are plucked one at a time. Chords played in this manner are called "arpeggios". There are many different kinds of arpeggio patterns. Sometimes they give a very lyrical quality to songs such as Greensleeves or Shenandoah. Other times they may enhance the rhythmic feeling of John Henry or a blues.

You may have heard the word "picking" in reference to one or another style of guitar (or banjo) playing - "Travis picking," "Scruggs picking," "southern picking"...Not all these terms mean precisely the same thing to everyone who uses them but of one thing you can be sure: The player is using his fingers to pluck some strings individually as part of some simple or complex rhythmic pattern.

So...try this: Play the bass string...then pluck the third string with your first finger...then pluck the second string with your second finger...then pluck the first string with your third finger...

Now try it again.

Now try this: First play a "regular" strum, consisting of "bass-chord" and then follow with the arpeggio. Make sure that the faster "one-and-two-and" of the arpeggio takes the same time to play as the "one-two" of the "bass-chord".

You may also alternate basses and play runs while using arpeggios:

GOING DOWN THE ROAD

I'M GOIN' DOWN THE ROAD FEEL-ING

BAD OH LORD I'M GOIN' DOWN THE ROAD FEEL-ING

BAD I'M GOIN' DOWN THE ROAD FEEL-ING

BAD, LORD LORD AND I AIN'T GON-NA BE TREATED THISA

- WAY

I'm going where the climate suits my clothes (3 times)
And I ain't gonna be treated thisaway.

I'm tired of lying in this jail...

I'm going where the water tastes like wine...
'Cause this prison water tastes like turpentine.

Two dollar shoes hurt my feet...

Ten dollar shoes suit me fine...

I'm goin where the chilly winds don't blow...

* * * * * * * * * * * * * * * * * * * *

Basic arpeggios in $\frac{3}{4}$ time are played thus:

Thumb - bass string
1st finger - 3rd string
2nd finger - 2nd string
3rd finger - 1st string
2nd finger - 2nd string
1st finger - 3rd string

The six beats of the arpeggio ("one-and-two-and-three-and") take the same time as the original "oom-pah-pah" ("one-two-three").

WHO'S GONNA SHOE
YOUR PRETTY LITTLE FOOT

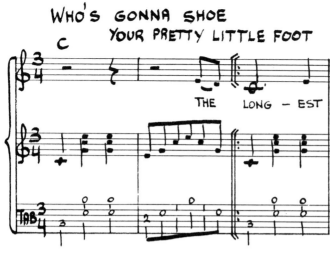

THE LONG-EST

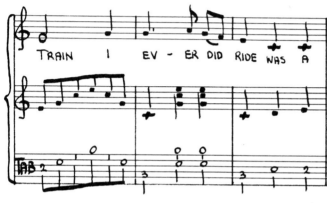

TRAIN I EV-ER DID RIDE WAS A

HUN-DRED COACH-ES LONG

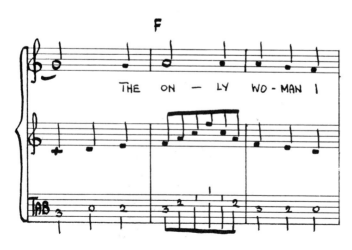

THE ON-LY WO-MAN I

EV-ER DID LOVE WAS ON THAT

TRAIN AND GONE

On that train and gone
On that train and gone
The only woman I ever did love
Was on that train and gone.

Who's gonna shoe your pretty little foot?
Who's gonna glove your hand?
Who's gonna kiss your red ruby lips?
Who's gonna be your man?

Who's gonna be your man?
Who's gonna be your man?
Who's gonna kiss your red ruby lips?
Who's gonna be your man?

Well, papa's gonna shoe my pretty little foot,
Mama's gonna glove my hand,
And sister's gonna kiss my red ruby lips,
I don't need no man.

I don't need no man,
I don't need no man,
Sister's gonna kiss my red ruby lips -
I don't need no man.

ON TOP OF OLD SMOKY

ON TOP OF OLD SMO —

— KY ALL COV-ERED WITH

SNOW LOST MY TRUE

LOV — ER FROM A-

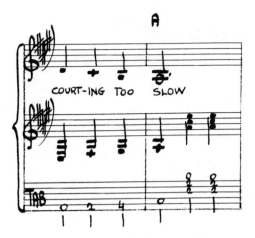

COURT-ING TOO SLOW

Well, a-courting's a pleasure,
And parting is grief.
But a false-hearted lover
Is worse than a thief.

A thief he will rob you
And take all you have.
But a false-hearted lover
Will send you to your grave.

And the grave will decay you
And turn you to dust.
And where is the young man
A poor girl can trust.

They'll hug you and kiss you
And tell you more lies
Than the cross-ties on the railroad,
Or the stars in the skies.

They'll tell you they love you
Just to give your heart ease.
But the minute your back's turned,
They'll court whom they please.

So come all you young maidens
And listen to me.
Never place your affection
On a green willow tree.

For the leaves they will wither
And the roots they will die,
And your true love will leave you,
And you'll never know why.

HAMMERING-ON

It is possible to get some notes striking a string very sharply with a finger of the left hand. This technique - hammering on - is a very useful one in many different kinds of songs.

We'll try several different "hammerings on".....

Finger a C chord. Now lift the 2nd finger off the 4th string and play the 4th string. Then hammer the 2nd finger back on to the 2nd fret. Now combine it with a regular strum like this:

Similarly with F and G7;

And here's what you do with E, D, A and B7;

Hammering on may be combined with all your other previously learned techniques (alternating bass, runs and arpeggios) as follows:

THIS LAND IS YOUR LAND
by Woody Guthrie

As I went walking that ribbon of highway
I saw above me that endless skyway,
I saw below me that golden valley –
This land was made for you and me.

I roamed and rambled and followed my footsteps
To the sparkling sands of her golden desert,
And all around me a voice was sounding,
This land was made for you and me.

When the sun come shining, then I was strolling
With the wheat fields waving and the dust clouds
    rolling,
And voice was chanting as the fog was lifting –
This land was made for you and me.

35

You don't have to put everything you know into every song you play - much of best in folk music consists of tasteful understatement and a "restricted palette" of colors - but these examples just give you an idea of what could be done.

EAST VIRGINIA

G^7

AND WHOSE NAME

C

I DID NOT KNOW

etc

Well, her hair was dark of color,
Cheeks they were a rosy red.
On her breast she wore white lillies,
Where I longed to lay my head.

I'd rather live in some dark holler
Where the sun would never shine,
Than for you to love another,
And to know you'd never be mine.

I don't want your greenback dollar,
I don't want your silver chain;
All I want is your love darling,
Say that you'll be mine again.

* * * * * * * * * * * * * * * * * * * *

THE FLAT PICK AND THE CHURCH LICK

If you have a steel-string guitar you would do well
to learn how to use a flat-pick. Nylon strung instruments
just don't respond well to pick playing.

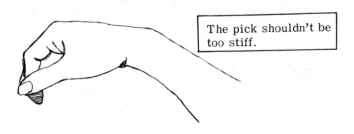

The pick shouldn't be
too stiff.

With the pick grasped firmly but flexibly between the
thumb and the forefinger just try strumming "bass-
chord" the way you did it away back when you played
only with your thumb. Try alternating basses. You may
run into difficulty hitting the string you want to until you
get used to the feel of the pick. That shouldn't take too
long. Don't bang the strings too hard - that's not the
main purpose of using a pick.

When playing with a flat pick you'll find a nice rhythmic strum is achieved by striking the chord on the way
up as well as the way down. Woody Guthrie used to call
it the "church-lick" and he used it to play many of the
songs which he heard recorded by the famous country
music group the Carter Family, back during the 1930's.

Play an E chord.

Pick the bass string - then all the rest (down). Then
come back up over the strings.

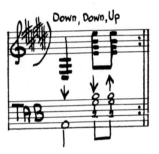

Down, Down, Up

THE CHURCH LICK WITH THE BLUES WRINKLE

Many of the songs of Woody Guthrie, the Carter Family, Jimmie Rodgers and others have blues feeling (if they are not actually blues) and sound particularly well when played with this strum.

Finger an E major chord and play "bass-down bass-up-down-up" in the following rhythmic pattern:

Make sure that the "and" after "3" is an upstroke.

After you get this pattern running smoothly try lifting the first finger (left hand) off the G string on "4" and putting it back on the following "and".

On the A chord you'll have to revise your fingering a bit to get this blues wrinkle to sound.

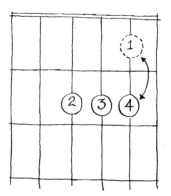

Keep your first finger on the first fret of the B string and lift the pinky off on "4" and replace it on "and".

Now let's try <u>Mule Skinner Blues</u>...

MULE SKINNER BLUES

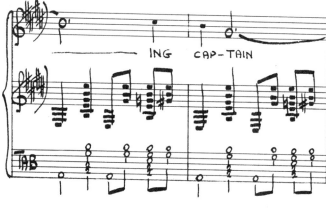

38

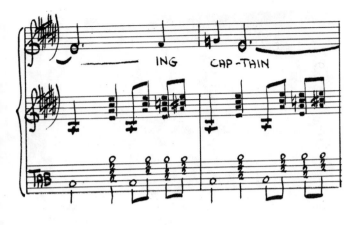

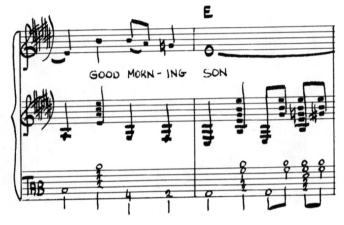

Well, I like to work - I'm rolling all the time,
Yes, I like to work - I'm rolling all the time.
I can pop my initials right on the mule's behind.

Well it's, Hey little water boy, bring your water 'round
Hey little water boy bring your water 'round.
If you don't like your job set that water bucket down.

I'm a-working on the new road at a dollar and a dime
    a day,
Working on that new road at a dollar and a dime a day.
I got three women waiting on a Saturday night just to
    draw my pay.

* (See Carter family technique, p. 40)

THE CARTER FAMILY

The singing Carter Family of Virginia - under the leadership of A.P. Carter - achieved national prominence shortly after their first RCA Victor recording session in August 1927. In a recording career that spanned three decades their individual style of playing and singing, as well as the songs, themselves, have had a tremendous influence on folk and country musicians. A partial list of Carter Family songs includes such favorites as Worried Man Blues, I never Will Marry, The Wabash Cannonball, John Hardy...and Wildwood Flower.

Characteristically, their guitar playing combined aspects of what we have called the church lick, the blues wrinkle hammering on and bass runs (played with a pick).

In the key of C we'll be using the same church-lick rhythmic pattern:

But the wrinkle comes on "3 - and" like this:

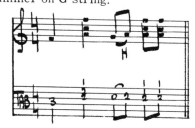

For F - hammer on G string:

And for G$_7$ - hammer on A string

WILDWOOD FLOWER

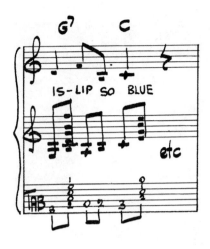

Oh he promised to love me,
He promised to love,
And to cherish me always
All others above.
I woke from my dream
And my idol was clay.
My passion for loving
Had vanished away.

Oh, he taught me to love him,
He called me his flower,
A blossom to cheer him
Through life's weary hour.
But now he is gone
And left me alone,
The wild flowers to weep
And the wild birds to mourn.

I'll dance and I'll sing
And my life shall be gay,
I'll charm every heart
In the crowd I survey;
Though my heart now is breaking,
He never shall know
How his name makes me tremble,
My pale cheeks to glow.

I'll dance and I'll sing
And my heart will be gay,
I'll banish this weeping
Drive troubles away.
I'll live yet to see him
Regret this dark hour,
When he won and neglected
This frail wildwood flower.

CARTER FAMILY

MORE ARPEGGIOS

The basic arpeggios that we discussed on page *30* are by no means the only kind of arpeggios that can be played. Any combination of notes played within a particular chord is by definition an arpeggio. If you are playing a slower-moving more lyrical piece the "one-two three-and-four-and" pattern will not do.

Try this:

In this arpeggio all the beats are evenly spaced.

Here's a new (and better) way of playing E7. Use t from now on whenever E7 is called for.

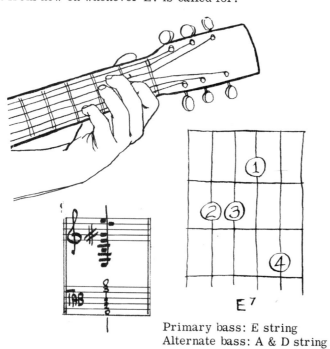

Primary bass: E string
Alternate bass: A & D string

TENTING TONIGHT

WE'RE TENT-ING TO-NIGHT ON THE

OLD CAMP GROUND   GIVE US A SONG TO

CHEER   OUR   WEA — RY HEARTS A

SONG OF HOME   AND FRIENDS WE LOVE SO

We've been tenting tonight on the old camp ground,
Thinking of days gone by,
Of the loved ones at home that gave us the hand,
And the tear that said, "Goodbye". (Cho.)

We are tired of war on the old camp ground,
Many are dead and gone,
Of the brave and true who've left their homes,
Others been wounded long. (Cho.)

We've been fighting today on the old camp ground,
Many are lying near
Some are dead and some are dying,
Many are in tears.(Cho.)

* * * * * * * * * * * * * * * * * * * *

43

Not all arpeggios are evenly spaced. Very often a pattern such as this will be used:

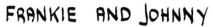

In the above pattern the first beat of each group of two notes is held longer (3 or 4 times longer) than the second. It produces a "bluesy" or a "boogie-woogie" feeling. (More on this later.)

FRANKIE AND JOHNNY

FRAN-KIE AND JOHN-NY WERE LO-VERS

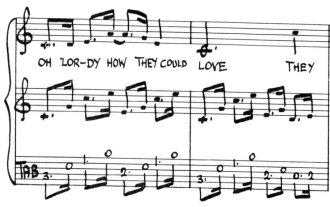

OH 'LOR-DY HOW THEY COULD LOVE   THEY

SWORE TO BE TRUE TO EACH O-THER

TRUE AS THE STARS A — BOVE, HE WAS HER
MAN   BUT HE DONE HER
WRONG   etc

Frankie and Johnny went walking,
Johnny in his brand-new suit.
"Oh, good Lord," said Frankie,
"Don't my Johnny-man look cute."
He was her man, but he done her wrong.

Johnny said, "I've got to leave you,
"But I won't be very long;
"Don't wait up for me, honey,
"Or worry while I'm gone."
He was her man, but he done her wrong.

Frankie went down to the corner,
Went in the saloon for some beer.
She said to the fat bartender,
"Has my Johnny-man been here?"
He was her man, but he done her wrong.

44

"Well I won't tell you no story,
"And I won't tell you no lie,
"I saw your Johnny about an hour ago
"With a gal named Nellie Bly."
"If he's your man, he's doin' you wrong."

Oh, Frankie got off at South 12th Street,
Looked up in a window so high,
And there she saw her Johnny
A-hugging that Nellie Bly.
He was her man, but he was doing her wrong.

Frankie pulled out her six shooter,
Pulled out her old forty-four;
Her gun went root-a-toot-toot-toot,
And Johnny rolled over the floor.
He was her man, but he done her wrong.

"Oh, roll me over so easy,
"Oh, roll me over so slow;
"Oh, roll me over easy, boys,
"For my wounds they hurt me so;
"I was her man, but I done her wrong."

Roll out your rubber-tired carriage,
Oh, roll out your old-time hack;
There's twelve men going to the graveyard,
And eleven coming back.
He was her man but he done her wrong.

* *

TWO-FINGER PICKING

It is possible to play a melody on the top strings with the first (or other) finger and at the same time keep the bass going with your thumb.

First, start a good strong pattern going with your thumb:

At the same time your right index finger plucks on the 1st and 2nd strings:

SKIP TO MY LOU

Sometimes these melody notes can be on the beat that is, coinciding with the thumb beat like they were just now, but often a folk musician will play some on and some off the beat between thumb beats. Also, the thumb doesn't have to strike a full chord each time but may alternate from string to string, playing chords ad libitum.

SKIP TO MY LOU

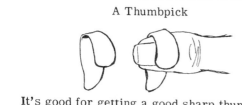

A Thumbpick

It's good for getting a good sharp thump out of the bass strings..

RAILROAD BILL

Some folk musicians use their right middle finger, as well as index finger, for the melody notes.

FREIGHT TRAIN

as played by
ELIZABETH COTTON
Trans. Walter RAIM

47

A FAST "BANJO" STRUM

Finger an A chord.

1. Strike the bass note (A)
2. Brush lightly downward with fingernails over the rest of the strings.
3. Brush lightly upward with the first finger over the first couple of strings.
   (It doesn't matter here how many you strike.)

The rhythm looks like this:

If you're not sure how this rhythmic pattern sounds, try saying

This is the way a 5-string banjo often sounds - though not played quite this way.

You'll need to know E minor for this next song. Look it up in the back.

48

Em

OF - FI -CERS ARE COM-ING   FOR TO

A

TEAR YOUR   STILL   HOUSE   DOWN   etc

The first time I seen Darling Cory,
She was standing on the banks of the sea.
She had a pistol strapped 'round her bosom,
And a banjo on her knee.

Go 'way from me, Darling Cory,
Quit hanging around my bed.
Pretty women have run me distracted,
Corn likker's gone to my head.

Oh no oh no my darling,
I'll do the best I can.
I'll get me another woman -
You can hunt you another man.

Dig a hole, dig a hole in the meadow
A hole in the cold, cold ground.
Go and dig me a hole in the meadow,
For to lay darling Cory down.

⁶⁄₈ TIME

There is one other basic meter in "common use." Particularly in songs from the British Isles (or American songs derived from that tradition) do we find this so-called "compound meter". "Compound" because the six eighth notes which make up each measure may be divided into either two groups of three eighths.

or three groups of two eighths.

In the latter case $\left(\text{♫♫♫}\right)$ ⁶⁄₈ may be thought of as equivalent in feeling to ¾ time and may be played accordingly

The first instance $\left(\text{♫♫}\right)$ however, presents an entirely "new sound". The accent here falls on the first eighth note of each group of three

and an arpeggio involving the thumb, first and second finger suggests itself immediately:

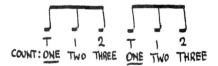

It is most often played at a rather fast pace as in The Wee Cooper O'Fife:

You'll need to know A minor for this next song. Look it up in the back.

THE WEE COOPER O'FIFE

50

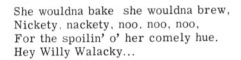

She wouldna bake she wouldna brew,
Nickety, nackety, noo, noo, noo,
For the spoilin' o' her comely hue.
Hey Willy Walacky...

She wouldna card, she wouldna spin,
Nickety, nackety, noo. noo, noo,
For the shamin' o' her gentle kin.
Hey Willy Walacky...

She wouldna wash, she wouldna wring,
Nickety, nackety, noo, noo, noo,
For the spoilin' o' her golden ring,
Hey Willy Walacky...

The cooper has gone to his wool pack,
Nickety nackety, noo, noo, noo,
He laid a sheep skin across his wife's back.
Hey Willy Walacky...

I wouldna thrash ye for your gentle kin,
Nickety, nackety, noo, noo, noo,
But I will thrash my own sheep skin.
Hey Willy Walacky...

A' ye wha hae gotten a gentle wife,
Nickety nackety, noo, noo, noo,
Send ye for the Wee Cooper O' Fife.
Hey Willy Walacky...

* *

The first two eighth notes of either or both of the groups of three may be combined:

ONE TWO THREE   ONE TWO THREE

(In this case "one two" is played by the thumb and "three" is a basic plucking with the fingers).

Try this pattern in Paddy Works on the Railway:

T   CHORD T   1   2
COUNT: ONE TWO THREE FOUR FIVE SIX

PADDY WORKS ON THE RAILWAY

IN   EIGHT-EEN HUN-DRED AND

FOR-TY ONE I PUT MY COR-DU-ROY

BRIT - CHES ON I PUT MY COR-DU-ROY

BRIT-CHES ON TO WORK UP-ON THE

G

OO - RI AYE TO WORK UP-ON THE

Am
RAIL — WAY

Am
RAIL — WAY

CHORUS
FI-LI-ME OO-RI

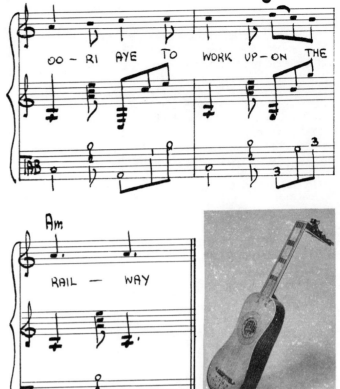

C
OO - RI AYE FI-LI-ME OO-RI

In eighteen hundred and forty-two
I left the old world for the new
Bad cess to the luck that brought me that brought me
    through,
To work upon the railroad. (Cho.)

In eighteen hundred and forty-three,
'Twas then I met sweet Biddy McGee,
An elegant wife she's been to me,
While working on the railroad. (Cho.)

It's, ''Pat, do this'', and ''Pat, do that'',
Without a stocking or cravat,
And nothing but an old straw hat,
While working on the railway. (Cho.)

In eighteen hundred and forty-six,
They pelted me with stones and sticks,
Oh, I was in a terrible fix,
While working on the railway. (Cho.)

In eighteen hundred and forty-seven,
Sweet Biddy McGee, she went to heaven.
If she left one child she left eleven,
To work upon the railway. (Cho.)

Am
OO - RI AYE FI-LI-ME OO-RI

BLUES

It is in the area of blues, perhaps more than in any other idiom, that the American folk guitarist has developed and perfected his technique into a high and personal art.

Aside from a few "academic" definitions of blues terminology (like: what is a blues?) and a few "sterile" specimens presented here, there is but one way to learn to play THE BLUES - and that is by listening, listening, listening to blues, blues, blues... In this respect the discography on page 78 is of the utmost importance.

In its most basic form a folk blues has

      a three-line stanza,
      a twelve-measure melody and
      three or four simple chords.

In its most refined form it is a free rhythmic, melodic, harmonic and lyric expression of a particular performer's innermost feelings at one specific time - that time coinciding with the performance.

Of necessity we will here concern ourselves with basics.

Modifying the strum illustrated on page 44 for Frankie and Johnny, try this:

GOOD MORNING BLUES

54

After you've done that a couple of times try this "walking bass" (boogie-woogie) in exactly the same rhythm:

GOOD MORNING BLUES

By this time you have undoubtedly noticed that each phrase ends "one measure too soon" - at the third measure. This means that out of each four measure phrase there might be only two measures of singing. That leaves two measures free for

PLAYING IN THE HOLES

Often this is best accomplished with two guitars (and two guitarists). One instrument plays the walking bass while the other fills in the holes:

GOOD MORNING BLUES

Got up this morning, blues
   walking 'round my bed.
   (2 times)
I went to eat my breakfast -
   the blues were all in my
   bread.

I sent for you yesterday -
   here you come a-walking
   today (2 times)
You got your mouth wide
   open, you don't know
   what to say.

Good morning, blues -
   blues how do you do
   (2 times)
I'm doin' all right - good
   morning, how are you?

* * * * * * * * * * * * * * * * * * * *

56

SOME BLUES EFFECTS

One of the most typical blues guitar effects is gotten by pulling the string with a finger of the left hand as you press on it. This stretches the string and raises the pitch a little. Then as you release the "pull" the string returns to its normal pitch.

Known as "choking" the string

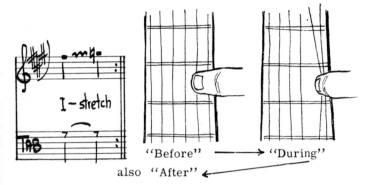

"Before" ——→ "During"

also "After" ←——

(The string can either be pulled down or pushed up. The effect will be the same.)

Now you can do that all through the blues.....

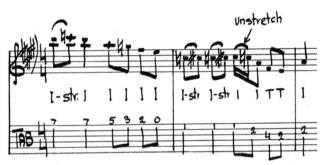

It's easily done on the top strings, but you can do it on the bass strings too.....

Other ways you can get slides is to press your finger down. Try it say on the second string, second fret....

And keep your finger pressed down, but move up the fingerboard three frets. ..
Try it again.   Then you can come down....

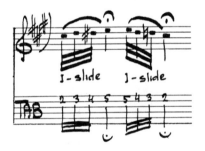

Now between these different things you can get a more fluid melody than if you just play the bare notes....

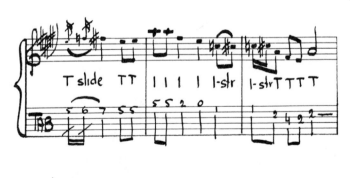

ANOTHER BLUES STRUM

Finger an E chord.

Part 1

The thumb strikes the sixth string and then brushes rapidly downward across the rest of the strings. As the thumb moves across the strings, the wrist, which is normally arched, is lowered until the heel of the hand is brought into contact with the vibrating strings, thereby muffling them. The rhythmic figure produced by this part of the strum is

Part 2

At the beginning of the second half of this pattern, the right hand which has moved vertically downward across the strings, now moves rapidly upward as the first finger brushes over the strings (highest note first; lowest, last). Then, either the thumb or the finger nails are brought rapidly downward over the strings again with the same muffling motion of the wrist. This completes the cycle

and we are ready to begin again.

The whole pattern looks like this:

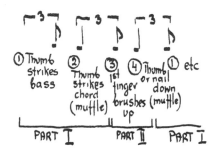

If you're not sure what the rhythm sounds like, sing (to yourself) The Worms Crawl In, The Worms Crawl Out:

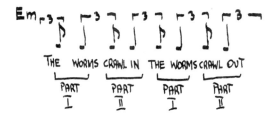

Better - listen to Josh White sing almost any of his blues*....Like Number 12 Train

---

* For learning more about blues history and theory as well as for many more blues you might like to glance at the book Folk Blues, by Jerry Silverman (pub. Macmillan Co.) One of the useful features of this book is that the piano arrangements - having been done by a guitarist - abound in typical guitar runs, breaks and hole-filler-uppers.

NUMBER 12 TRAIN

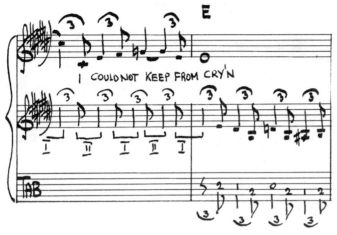

I COULD NOT KEEP FROM CRY'N

SOME-TIMES I'M NOT MY — SELF

SOMETIMES I FEEL I'M DY — IN'

Now from here on, you're really on your own. Remember that great musicians have spent their entire lives playing nothing but the Blues!

She left me all night long, I could not help myself (2 times)
I thought she was loving me - I found she had somebody
  else

I may be wrong but I'll be right some day (2 times)
But the next gal I get will have to do what poppa say.

* * * * * * * * * * * * * * * * * * * *

59

CALYPSO

West Indian music has recently become very popular in this country - and notwithstanding the fact that most calypsonians sing to the accompaniment of wind and percussion bands, many North American calypsonians use the guitar. The underlying musical feature of the West Indian calypso - the rhythmic syncopation - is grist for the guitarists' mill.

What is Syncopation?

Literally it is putting the ac-<u>cent</u> on the wrong syl-<u>lable</u>.

To the guitarist it means playing a beat where none would ordinarily occur - or, <u>not playing</u> a beat where one is expected. Sometimes the former implies the latter.

A simple illustration of this would be:

Play a simple four-downstroke strum-

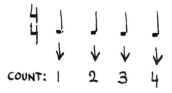

Now just leave out the third beat.

If you do this over and over giving the second beat a slightly heavier accent than normal you'll begin to hear the syncopation. Let the second stroke sound for two counts.

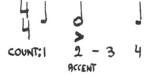

Now let's add a couple of more beats and get the fingers into the act

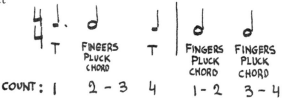

Usually when this strum is played the time values of each of the notes is actually one half of what was given above. However the relationship between the various components of the strum remains the same. To wit:

JOHN B.

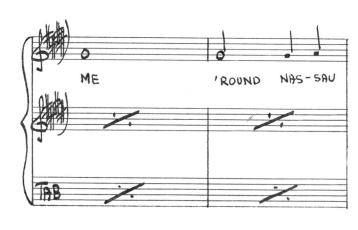

Chorus:

So hoist up the John B. sails
See how the mainsail sets
Send for the captain ashore
Let me go home, let me go home
I feel so break up
I want to go home.

The first mate, oh, he got drunk,
Broke up the people's trunk,
Constable had to come and take him away.
Sheriff Johnstone please leave me alone,
I feel so break-up - I want to go home. (Cho.)

The poor cook, oh, he got fits,
Ate up all of the grits.
Then he took and threw away all of the corn.
Sheriff Johnstone please leave me alone,
This is the worst trip I ever been on. (Cho.)

* * * * * * * * * * * * * * * * * * * *

If you play the eight eighth notes that make up a measure of $\frac{4}{4}$

and then join the fourth and fifth eighth notes

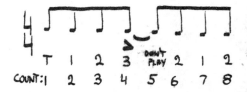

you have a nice relaxed Calypso strum.

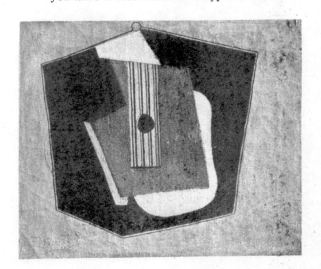

61

DELIA

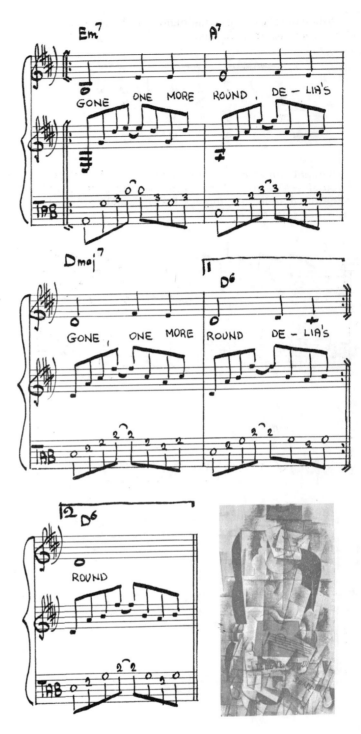

Send for the doctor - the doctor came too late.
Send for the minister to lay out Delia straight.

Delia, oh, Delia, where you been so long?
Everybody's talking about poor Delia's dead and gone.

Rubber-tired carriage - old-time broken hack
Took poor Delia to the graveyard but didn't bring her
  back.

* * * * * * * * * * * * * * * * * * * *

You can take those same eight eighth notes and divide them up another way:

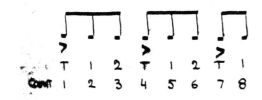

This strum sounds particularly good with a C chord if you alternate your thumb from the fifth to the fourth to the third string - and pluck the first and second strings with your fingers;

PAY ME MY MONEY DOWN

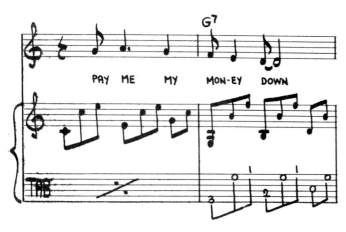

PAY ME, OH, PAY ME —

PAY ME MY MON-EY DOWN

PAY ME OR GO TO JAIL —

PAY ME MY MON-EY DOWN — I

THOUGHT I HEARD THE CAP-TAIN SAY —

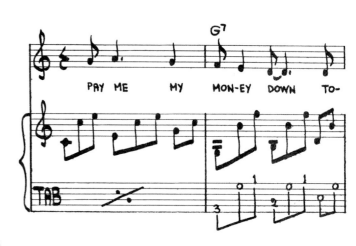

PAY ME MY MON-EY DOWN TO-

MOR- ROW IS OUR SAIL- ING DAY

PAY ME MY MON-EY DOWN.__

The very next day we cleared the bar,
    Pay me my money down,
He knocked me down with the end of a spar,
    Pay me my money down.   (Chorus)

I wish I was Mr. Howard's son,
    Pay me my money down,
Sit in the house and drink good rum,
    Pay me my money down.   (Chorus)

I wish I was Mr. Steven's son,
    Pay me my money down,
Sit on the bank and watch the work done,
    Pay me my money down.   (Chorus)

Another way of getting the same rhythm -

First brush down across all strings with the back
of your fingernails . . Follow down with your wrist and
strum across all strings with your thumb... Now strum
up across all strings with your index finger. .Now repeat
those three strokes again . . .Down...Down again with
your thumb. . And up. . .Finally brush down with your
fingernails and up with your index finger.....

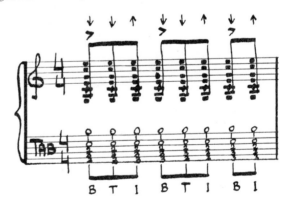

B T I   B T I   B I

DO IT YOURSELF

You can have a good time developing your own
"Calypso strums" by playing different combinations
of the eighth notes and varying the right hand with plucking chords bass notes arpeggios and brushing up and
down.

etc.

65

OTHER TUNINGS

While the customary tuning of guitars is the one you've been using up till now it is by no means the only one   Sometimes just one string is changed for a special effect in playing a song. For example supposing you try lowering your sixth string from E....down to D....

Now it's an octave lower than your fourth string.

Now if you'll check with the diagram, and start off with this rather interesting way of getting a D chord, here's one song you could use this with....

D A D G B E

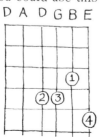

TIME'S A-GETTING HARD, BOYS

TIME'S A-GET-TING HARD, BOYS,

Take my Bible from the bed, shotgun from the wall.
Take Old Sal and hitch her up, the wagon for to haul.
Pile the chairs and beds up high, let nothing drag the ground;
Sal can pull and we can push - we're bound to leave this town.

Made a crop a year ago - it withered to the ground.
Tried to get some credit but the banker turned me down.
Goin' to Californ - I - ay, where everything is green,
Goin' to have the best farm that you have ever seen.

* *

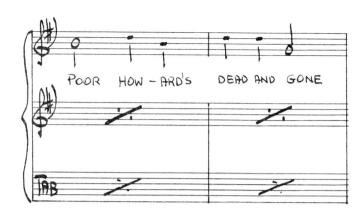

Another common way to retune the guitar is to lower the 6th, 5th and 1st strings each a whole tone. The guitar would then be tuned to an "open" G chord:

6	5	4	3	2	1
D	G	D	G	B	D

In this tuning a major chord can be played at any fret simply by laying the index finger across all the strings at that fret. Play C on the 5th fret and D on the 7th fret.

Who's been here since I've been gone) twice
Pretty little girl with a red dress on)

Pretty little girl with a red dress on (four times)

Who's been here since I've been gone) twice
Great big man with a derby on)

Great big man with a derby on (four times)

* * * * * * * * * * * * * * * * * * *

THE BARRE

The barre (pronounced "bar") is usually the index finger of the left hand which presses down tightly over all six strings at a particular fret and enables the remaining three fingers to play a chord. Barre chords are as necessary to a guitarist's technique as "non-barre" chords. Indeed, a chord is a chord is a chord - no matter where it may be found.

To play a barre properly it is necessary for the index finger to remain relatively rigid - at least, not to bend. Any undue curvature in the finger will mean that consistent pressure is not being maintained upon all the strings - and that ain't good!

One startling fact about a barre chord is that you get eleven for the price of one. If you learn, for example, these four patterns (two major, two minor - there are others) you will have added 44 new chords to your collection!

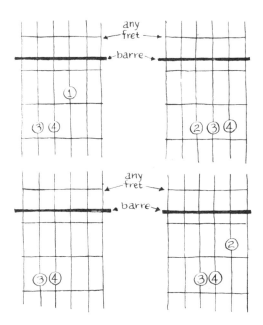

Check the chord page to find out what these chords are.

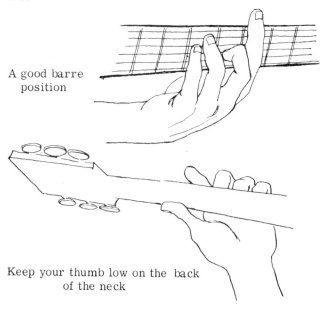

A good barre position

Keep your thumb low on the back of the neck

THE CAPO

Some day you may come across someone who sings Skip To My Lou in the key of E-flat (Yes, there is such a key). It's not entirely unrealistic to expect a guitarist to be able to execute this little musical nicety. Or, perhaps someone might want to sing Joshua Fought The Battle of Jericho in the key of C minor. Again, this, too, can be done by learning to play in C minor. On the other hand playing comfortably in E flat or C minor might take several years of study and what do you do about those songs in the meantime?

What do you do...? You take your capo and you clamp it across the first fret of your guitar and you finger a D chord (counting up the proper number of frets from the capo) and voilà! E flat.

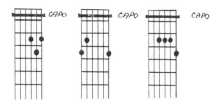

For C minor and its associated chords you would put the capo at the third fret and finger in the key of A minor.

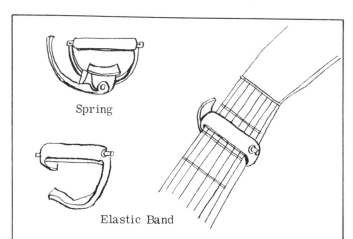

Spring

Elastic Band

Note: There are many different makes of capos on the market ranging in price from 50¢ to several dollars, and involving different types of springs, bands, and bars.

How would you play D flat? F sharp? A flat? G minor?

Here's how you figure it out - in case you haven't figured it out already. The capo raises the pitch of the guitar one half-step for each fret.

The half steps, starting from the low E string, proceed like this:

(Otherwise known as the chromatic scale)

So, to play in a key you don't know, merely look to the left (down the scale) of the unknown chord until you come to a chord you do know. Then count the number of notes (they're called "half steps") you've skipped and put the capo that many frets up the neck of the guitar. Now finger the familiar chord and there you have it.

So - D flat? Look back one to C. Capo goes on first fret and finger C = D flat.

———————————

If you have any doubts as to the morality of the use of the capo here is an article by Jerry Silverman on the subject reprinted from Volume 8, Number 1 (Spring 1958) of Sing Out:

THE CAPO - Guitarists' Boon or Bane?

The capo has had a long and honorable history. The word itself comes from the Italian capotasto, but its origins are much older and more diverse than, let us say, renaissance Italy - the source of so much of our musical terminology. For the uninitiated the capo (pr. kay' po) is a piece of metal or rubber (traditionally, wood or ivory) clamped over the fingerboard of the guitar to raise the pitch of all the strings simultaneously by an equal amount. Representations of different types of capos are to be found on ancient stone carvings of people playing stringed instruments, in paintings of different periods, and mention is made of them in books of instruction dealing with lutes, citterns, guitars, and other stringed instruments.

Despite this long, traditional use the guitarist who uses a capo today is very often the object of ridicule, or, at best, the butt of some sarcastic remark by a well-meaning, but uninformed member of the musical fraternity. A jazz guitarist, who does not use a capo, is apt to say to a folk guitarist who does, "Man, you mean you can't play in F-sharp minor?" A classical guitarist who shudders at the very idea of a capo may not even express his thoughts, but may smile condescendingly as if to say, "Oh well, what's the use - obviously no technique at all." Other musicians refer to the capo as a "crutch" or "cheater".

Even many folk guitarists who use capos and recognize their value have developed guilt feelings brought on by this constant barrage of criticism.

What answers are there to these critics? Are there any answers at all? I believe that there are - and sound musical ones at that.

We must examine the objectives of the folk guitarist as distinguished from those of his jazz and classical colleagues.

The crux of the matter lies in the fact that in most cases the folk guitarist's choice of key will be determined by the vocal range of the performer, a situation only sometimes encountered by the jazzman and never by the classicist. Then, it must be noted that traditional vocal accompaniment demands the legato quality of open-string chords merging and blending with each other rather than the staccato beat of the dance-band guitar. With a dance-band guitarist a capo would get in the way because he purposely avoids playing open strings in order to be able to achieve his desired effect: a steady, clipped beat. Ask him to play, say, Greensleeves, in F-sharp minor and see what happens. He'll play all the right chords but it will come out sounding like The Tennessee Waltz. Ask him to play a flowing accompaniment while his first finger is glued across all the strings at the second fret and you will probably get a pained look. It's not his fault. He may be any excellent guitarist but you just can't do without open strings if you want to have a sustained folk sound.

The classical guitarist is even easier to dispose of. Just ask him in what key he played that Bach prelude. When he tells you, "A major", remind him gently that the original key of the piece was probably B flat and Segovia (or whoever made the transcription) - being a realist - transposed the thing to A for ease in playing. This is exactly what the capo does. The difference is that the folk guitarist has the additional problem of vocal range and so he must suit the guitar to the voice and then the fingering (if it comes out in an awkward key) to the guitar. The classical guitarist, with no such vocal problem, merely transposes the piece to the easiest playing key. You don't see the capo when Segovia plays, but it's there all the time.

Flamenco guitarists, whose technical virtuosity is unrivalled by any musicians' - Sabicas, Montoya, Escudero, and the rest - all accompany dancers and singers and, hence, all use capos as a matter of course.

Unquestionably, many less competent folk guitarists do use the capo as a convenient way out of somewhat difficult situations. But the mere use of the capo does not in itself indicate incompetence. There is no substitute for learning to play chords like F-sharp minor and B flat and all the rest. At any moment, in any piece in any key you may be called upon to play a chord involving a barre or a relatively unfamiliar fingering pattern. A capo cannot help you there, but it would be equally foolhardy for a folk guitarist to start a piece in one of these awkward keys. A good guitarist is one who has learned from experience and knows instinctively just when and when not to attach his capo.

Here's a musical bonus for working so hard and doing so well.

THE MEXICAN BLUES   (by Pete Seeger)

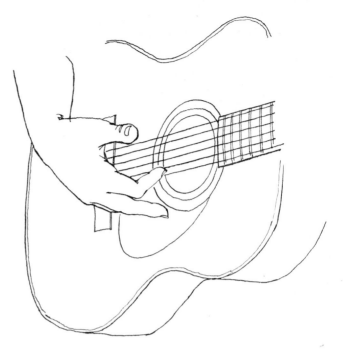

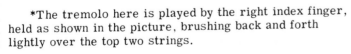

+o BEGINNING

*The tremolo here is played by the right index finger, held as shown in the picture, brushing back and forth lightly over the top two strings.

The little finger and the ring finger are braced against the guitar. The thumb is braced against the joint of the index finger, high enough so that the latter can move freely. The middle finger can wiggle uselessly if it so wishes.

ON THE BUYING OF A GUITAR...

Even on this seemingly most basic question there is a variety of opinion. The question is not only one of what brand to acquire and how much to spend but also the seemingly perplexing problem of the nylon-strung (classical) guitar versus the steel-strung flat top guitar. The authors (and their friends) not being 100% in agreement we feel it best to present three somewhat concurring, somewhat conflicting and somewhat confusing statements on the subject.

The first is an article which appeared in Volume 1, Number 8 of Sing Out way back in January 1951.

....SO YOU WANNA BUY A GUITAR
An Authoratative Article
by Joe Jaffe

If you want to get a decent instrument, you'll have to buy a new Martin or Gibson* or one of the hand-made Spanish varieties ranging from sixty-five up to a few thousand dollars. If you have the dough, swell - don't read this article; it's intended for the poorer class.

At this point someone tells me skeptically that they've seen good guitars for $5, $10, $15. "Why, they have strings and all, bright colors, and you can comb your hair in the shiny wood." Vehemently I reply that they represent a capitalistic plot to take in a large unsuspecting market. These "guitars" are made of inferior grain, unseasoned wood, sound tinny, would give Frankenstein sore fingers, and their hard, shiny varnish only kills the tone some more.

The solution is to get a second-hand instrument in some pawn shop or old instrument store. I'll tell you how to spot a good one before it falls into the clutches of those hateful enthusiasts who stuff their closets with instruments they never play.

First of all, we want to get the round-hole, flat-top guitar since this type has the most resonant sound. The f-hole variety only sounds good when electrically amplified and is usually found in swing-band playing. Now if you're lucky, you'll find a hand-made "classical" model. These are distinguished by a very wide and thin keyboard, a thin wood face and a characteristic bridge with horizontal string holes. These are the best of guitars and their playing gives real pleasure. Their appearance is usually duller due to the soft varnish used.

Look at the face of your guitar. It should have the close, straight grain of good spruce and is usually light-colored. The back and sides are usually of darker short-grained mahogany, or in the better models, of red-brown richly flowing-grain rosewood.

The keyboard on a good instrument is made of smooth, black ebony, though rosewood is used too. If there are two cut-out channels in the wood of the gear box, this alone will usually denote a good guitar.

The most important thing for beginners is the string action. You can always spot a cheap guitar since you

can put your hand in the space between the keyboard and the strings. The strings shouldn't be more than 1/8 inch from the keyboard or terrible blisters and frustration will ensue. If the action is bad due to warping, it sometimes pays to straighten out an obviously superior instrument. Action can be improved by filing down the notches on the nut and bridge and by changing the strings to the silk and steel variety.

Good Hunting!

This appeared in the first edition of The Folksinger's Guitar Guide by Pete Seeger:

HOW AND WHERE TO GET A GUITAR

A good new guitar - like any good musical instrument, is expensive. $25 up to several hundred dollars. If you are in a hurry, and can afford it, any music store will be glad to help you spend your money.

For accompanying yourself singing folk songs, steer clear of electric guitars, guitars with "f" holes in the sounding box, instead of a round hole, and instead, select a "Spanish" style guitar. Especially if you have never played a guitar, I'd suggest you start with nylon strings, even if later on you decide you prefer the twang of steel strings. Much easier on the finger-tips.

If you have time to poke around second hand stores, and if you have a guitar playing friend to accompany you, you might get a better buy. Be wary for following points: lay a straight edge (such as a ruler) along the fingerboard to determine if the neck is warped. Cracks can be mended but straightening a warped neck is a major operation, useless to attempt except in the case of an unusually fine instrument worth saving. See if all the frets are smooth and of even height. If the pegs don't turn easily, it will cost you a few dollars to replace them.

Listen to the tone of several dozen instruments, and you'll be able to tell which please you best. Some are weak in the bass notes, others weak in the high notes. Some are not loud at all, but still have a superlative quiet balance of tone.

When you have it, treat it as you would a violin; keep it dry, and don't put it near too much heat - as on top of a radiator. Remember, one drop on a hard floor will produce a crack expensive to mend. Change the strings when they get to sound too dull, and oil the tuning pegs to make them turn smoothly. (If the guitar has old fashioned wooden friction pegs, that is a separate problem. They're awfully tricky to use.)

* Since this article was written, several other guitar manufacturers have entered the folk music field, particularly Goya, Guild and Favilla.

To complete the trilogy we have part of a "Git Box" article from Volume 7, Number 3 (Fall 1957) of Sing Out by Jerry Silverman:

...SHOULD I BUY A NYLON OR STEEL STRING GUITAR?

This is a problem which generally confronts every prospective folk guitarist - and the choice is often a difficult one to make. Both types of strings have something to be said for and against them.

Nylon strung guitars are usually referred to as "classical" guitars. A classical guitar is distinguishable by its rather wide fingerboard, slotted tuning mechanism, flat top, round sound hole and a bridge with the string holes drilled parallel to the top of the guitar. A classical guitarist invariably uses his bare fingers to pluck the nylon (formerly gut) strings. The quality of the sound produced in this manner is somewhat on the delicate side, although Flamenco guitarists using similar instruments can achieve percussive effects by using their fingernails. Folk guitarists who use the classical guitar are limiting in advance the number of types of folksongs they can successfully attack.

By way of explanation, let us examine the steel string guitar. This guitar should also have a flat top and round sound hole. Its fingerboard is somewhat narrower than that of its classical cousin and the strings are generally attached to the bridge by pegs. This guitar can be played equally well with the bare fingers or with a variety of flat or finger picks. The quality of sound is more incisive and forceful.

Discounting a preference for the sound (timbre), what would make a prospective guitarist choose nylon over steel? After all, anything that can be played on nylon can be played on steel - and then some! Blues, hillbilly jazz group song leading - to name just a few - are some of the areas where a nylon string guitar cannot compete with steel.

The choice is often made for non-musical reasons: Insidious propaganda of the Nylon Trust has brainwashed the gullible populace into believing that steel string guitars are physically more difficult to play and that blood poisoning may occur from pressing down on rusty strings.

Our answer to that is, "Forsooth"! A <u>good</u> guitar is easy to manipulate - steel or nylon. That's the secret.

Get as good an instrument as you possibly can afford. There is a false economy in getting a cheap guitar if you are at all serious about studying.

And as far as the blood poisoning is concerned, most of the people recover anyway...

FINGERNAILS AND FINGER PICKS

In case you haven't noticed already it's of utmost importance that the fingernails of each hand be the right length.

Those of the left hand will have to be short, so the fingers can come down directly and firmly on the string, without the nail touching at all.

← FRETS →

Those on the right hand should be neither too long or too short. When plucking the flesh of the fingertip should touch the string first but the nail be last to leave it.

People who play a great deal of two-finger guitar picking often wear finger picks and thumbpicks to save their nails, and to get a crisper tone from the strings.

Hardly any two people like the exact same kind of picks. The kind we like looks like this:

If you don't like to use fingerpicks, but your nails break and tear, you might experiment with spreading a coat of Dupont cement on them, as reinforcement. Or a commercial preparation, such as 'Patti-Nail', is harder yet. But nothing stays on permanently.

75

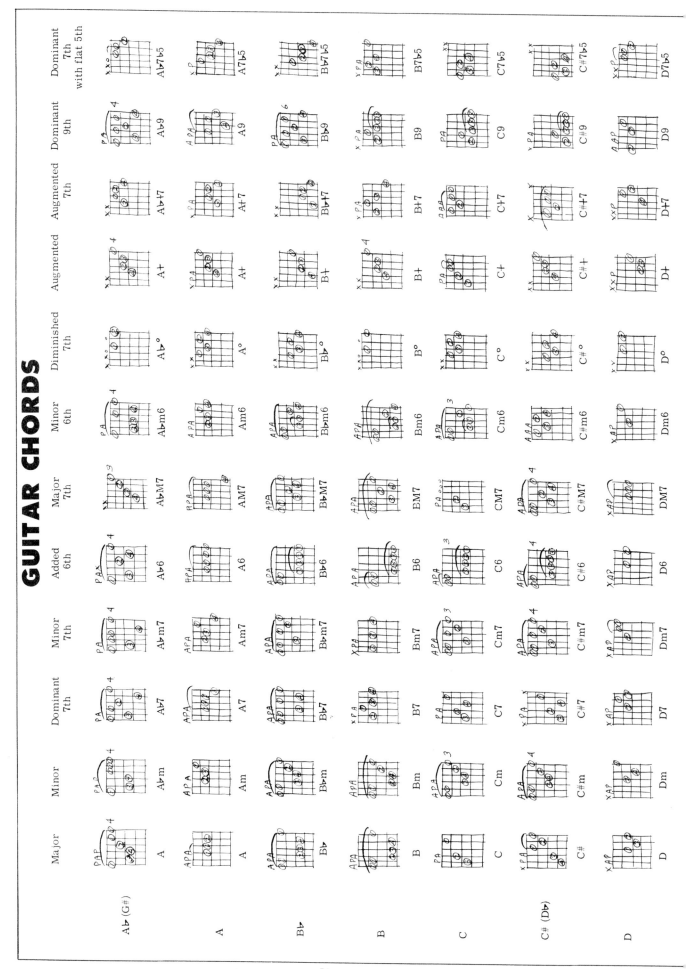

GUITAR CHORDS

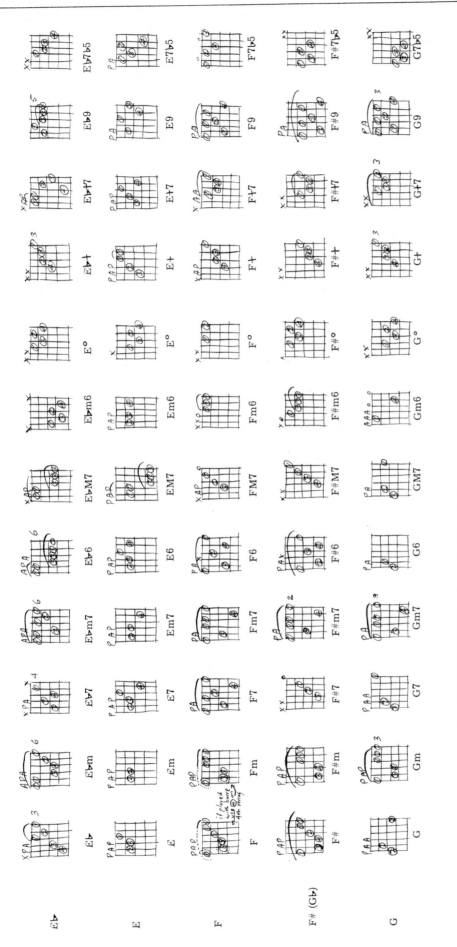

The following symbols are used in this chart:

P = Primary bass string

A = Alternate bass string

⌒ = Barre

╌⌒ = Optional barre

x = String not to be played

° = Open string to be played

The number to the right of some of the diagrams indicates the fret at which the chord is to begin.

The chord patterns given here present only one possible fingering for each chord. However, all of the barre chord patterns may be played at any fret (with one half-step change in pitch per fret) thus producing alternate fingerings for all the chords.

DISCOGRAPHY

The following discography offers a wide selection of music of interest to folk guitar players. Get familiar with as much of it as you can (afford). It's the best way to learn...

Badeaux, Ed -Am. Guitar	Folk 3534
Baez, Joan	Van 9078
Broonzy, Big Bill-Sings country blues	Folk 2326
Big Bill's Blues	Col WL-111
Blues	Mer. 36137
Last Session	3-Verve 3001/3
Songs & Story	Folk 3586
Story	5-Verve 3000-5
Broonzy, Terry, & McGhee	Folk 3817
Cat Iron-Blues & Hymns	Folk 2389
Clayton, Paul-Bay State Ballads	Folk 2106
Cumberland Mt. Folksongs	Folk 2007
Days of Moby Dick	Trad. 1005
Foc'sle Songs & Shanties	Folk 2429
Folk Ballads of English Speaking World	Folk 2310
Home-Made Songs & Ballads	Monu. 4001
Virginia Folk Songs & Ballads	Folk 2110
Unholy Matrimony	Elek. 147
Cotton, Eliz. -Negro Songs	Folk 3526
Country Blues-Jefferson Johnson, Carr, Estes, Broonzy, Washboard Sam	Folk RF-1
Country Gentlemen-Bluegrass	Folk 2409
Darling, Erik	Elek. 154
Davis, Blind Gary-Harlem Street Singers	Prest. Blues 1015
Davis, Rev. Gary-Gospel Blues	Riv. 148
Dyer-Bennet, Richard	
Dyer-Bennet 1	Dyer-Bennet 1000
Dyer-Bennet 2	Dyer-Bennet 2000
Dyer-Bennet 3	Dyer-Bennet 3000
Dyer-Bennet 4	Dyer-Bennet 4000
Dyer-Bennet 5	Dyer-Bennet 5000
Dyer-Bennet 9	Dyer-Bennet 9000 S-9000
Gems of Minstrelsy	Dyer-Bennet 8000
Elliot, Jack-Guthrie Songs	Prest. Int. 13016
Fuller, Jesse -Blues, Jazz, Spirituals & Folk Songs	GTJ 12031
Gerlach, Fred-12-String Guitar	Folk 3529
Guthrie, Woody-Bound for Glory	Folk 2481
Ballads of Sacco & Vanzetti	Folk 5485
Dust Bowl Ballads	Folk 2011
Hooker, John Lee -Country Blues	Riv. 838
Blues	King 727
I'm John Lee Hooker	Vee 1007
Plays & Sings the Blues	Chess 1454
That's my story	Riv. 321:1175
Travelin'	Vee 1023
Hopkins, Lightnin'	Folk 3822
Autobiography in Blues	Trad 1040
Country Blues	Trad 1035
In New York	Candid 8010
Last Night Blues w. Terry	Prest. Blues 1029
Lightnin	Prest. Blues 1019
Lightnin' & Blues	Herald 1012
Houston, Cisco - Hard Travelin'	Folk 2042
Cisco Special	Van 9057
Cisco Special	Van 2042
900 Miles & Other RR Ballads	Folk 2013
Sings Folk Songs	Folk 2346
Songs of Open Road	Folk 2480
Songs of Woody Guthrie	Van. VRS 9089
Jefferson, Blind Lemon -Folk-Blues	Riv 125
Vol. 2, Jazz & Blues	Riv 136

Johnson, Lonnie -Blues	Prest. Blues 1007
Blues & Ballads	" " 1011
Losing Game	" " 1024
Kazee, Buell-Songs & Music	Folk 3810
Lead Belly-Last Session	Folk 2941/2
Legacy	Folk 2004, 14, 24, 34
McGhee, Brownie -Blues	Folk 2030
Blues	Folk 3557
Traditional Blues	Folk 2421
Vol. 2	Folk 2422
McGhee & Terry-Back Country Blues	Savoy 14019
Blues & Folk	Prest. Blues 1005
Blues & Folksongs	Folk 2327
Blues Around My Head	Prest. Blues 1020
Blues Is a Story	World 1294;S-1294
Blues Is My Companion	Verve 3008;63008
Down Home Blues	Prest Blues 1007
Down Home Blues	Sharp 2003
Folk Songs	Rou. 25074
Just a Closer Walk With Thee	Fan 3296;8042
On the Road w. Burris	Folk 2369
Terry & McGhee	Fan 3254
Work, Play, Faith, Fun	Choice 100;100
Miller, Mickey	Folk 2393
Odetta-Sings Ballads & Blues	Trad. 1010
At Carnegie Hall	Van 9076; 2072
At the Gate of Horn	Trad;1025;2057
Ballad for Americans	Van 9066;2057
My Eyes Have Seen	Van 9059;2046
Odetta	Fan 3252
Rodgers, Jimmie - Never No Mo' Blues	Vic LPM-1232
Jimmie The Kid	Vic LPM-2213
My Rough & Rowdy Ways	Vic LPM-2112
Train Whistle Blues	Vic LPM-1640
Sandburg, Carl---Great	Lyr. 66
Flat Rock Ballads	Col. ML-5339
Seeger, Peggy, Penny, Barbara, Michael-Folk Songs	Folk 2005
Seeger, Peggy - Best	Prest.Int. 13005
Songs of Courting & Complaint	Folk 2049
Seeger, Pete - Ballads	Folk 2319
American Favorite Ballads	Folk. 2320
Vol. 2	Folk 2321
Vol. 3	Folk 2322
Vol. 4	Folk 2323
American Industrial Ballads	Folk 5251
At Carnegie Hall	Folk 2412
At Village Gate	Folk 2450
Champlain Valley Songbag	Folk 5210
Concert	Stinson 57
Darling Corey	Folk 2003
Frontier Ballads	2-10" Folk 2175/6 (5003)
Gazette	Folk 2501
Goofing-Off Suite	10" Folk 2045
Indian Summer - Soundtrack	Folk 3851
Love Songs for Friends & Foes	Folk 2453
Rainbow Design	Folk 2454
Sampler	10" Folk 2043
Sing Out	Folk 2455
Story Songs	Col. CL-1668;CS-8468
Talking Union	Folk 5285
With Voices Together We Sing	Folk 2452
Seeger, Cohen & Paley - New City Lost Ramblers	Folk 2396
Seeger & Hamilton - Nonesuch	Folk 2439
Silverman, Jerry - Folk Blues	AV 101 (Folk)
Sykes, Roosevelt	
Return	Prest. Blues 1006
Honeydripper	Prest. Blues 1014
Travis, Merle - Back Home	Cap. T-891
Walkin' the Strings	Cap. T-1391
Van Ronk, Dave - Ballads, Blues	Folk 3818
Waters, Muddy - Best	Chess 1427
At Newport 1960	Chess 1449
Weavers - At Carnegie Hall	Van. 9010
Vol. 2, April 1, 1960	Van. VRS-9075
At Home	Van. 9024;2030
Best	Dec. 8893
Folk Songs Around the World	Dec. 8909
Travelling On	Van. 9043;2022
Weavers On Tour	Van. 9013
White, Josh - And Big Bill Broonzy	Per. 1209
Blues	Mer. 20203
Chain Gang Songs	Elk. 158;7158
House I Live In	Elk. 203;7203
Josh	Elek. 114
Josh White (4-58)	Dec. 8665
Josh at Midnight	Elek. 102
Program	Lon. LL1341
Spirituals & Blues (2-61)	Elek. 193;7193
Stories	2-ABC 124,166
25th Anniversary Album	Elek. 123

Key to Record Labels		
	Mer.	Mercury
	Monu.	Monument
Cap.	Capitol	Per.	Period
Col.	Columbia	Prest.	Prestige
Dec.	Decca	Riv.	Riverside
Elek.	Elektra	Rou.	Roulette
Fan.	Fantasy	Trad.	Tradition
Folk.	Folkways	Van.	Vanguard
GTJ	Good Time Jazz	Vic.	RCA-Victor

BIBLIOGRAPHY

Here are some good collections of folk songs:

Best, Dick and Beth - Song Fest, Crown Pub. N.Y. paper ($1.95)

Bikel, Theo - Folksongs and Footnotes, Meridian Books, NY ($2.95)

Boni, Margaret - Fireside Book Of Folk Songs, Simon & Schuster, NY ($5.00)

Brand, Oscar - Folksongs For Fun, Berkeley Pub. NY paper (.60)

Cazden Norman - Abelard Song Book, Abelard, NY ($6.95)

Fowke, Edith - Canada's Story In Song, Gage, Toronto ($5.00)

Guthrie, Woody (1) American Folksong, Oak Pub. ($1.95) ed. Moe Asch.
    (2) California To The New York Island, Oak Pub. NY ($1.95) ed. Millard Lampell
    (3) Ballads of Sacco and Vanzetti, Oak Pub. ($1.50)

Ives, Burl - The Burl Ives Song Book, Ballantine, NY paper (.50)

Landeck, Beatrice Songs My True Love Sings, Marks, NY ($1.25)

Leadbelly Songbook, Oak Pub.

Lomax, John and Alan - Best Loved American Folk Songs, Gross & Dunlap, NY ($5.95)

Lomax, Alan - The Folk Songs Of North America, Doubleday, NY ($7.50)

Sandburg, Carl - The American Song Bag, Harcourt, Brace & Co. NY

Seeger, Pete - American Favorite Ballads, Oak Pub. ($1.95)

Silber Irwin - Songs Of The Civil War, Columbia Univ. Pres, NY ($7.50)

Silverman, Jerry in Folk Blues, Macmillan, NY ($6.95)
    (2) Russian Song Book, Random House, NY

Weavers' Song Book, Harper, NY ($5.95) ed. Bob DeCormier.

Peoples' Song Book, Oak. ($1.95) ed. Waldemar Hille

Lift Every Voice (2nd Peoples' Song Book), Oak ($1.50). ed. Irwin Silber

Sing Out - folk song magazine. Published 5 times yearly (sub. $2.50) 121 W. 47th St. NYC

Reprints from Sing Out! - Vols. 1 - 4. ($1.00 ea.) Oak Pub.

Reprints from People's Songs Bulletin ($1.95), Oak Pub.

Josh White Guitar Method with Ivor Maraints. Boosey & Hawkes. NY

PICTURE CREDITS

Cover Design by Ronald Clyne
    Photo by David Gahr

Title Page: Gwathmey

P. 4 Photo by John Cohen
P. 5 Elizabeth Cotton and Grandchildren
P. 11 Photo from the Library of Congress (John Cohen collection)
P. 13 Open Window with Pedestal Table, Pablo Picasso, 1919
P. 14 Lee Hays, center; Bob Claiborne, right
P. 16 Earl Robinson
P. 17 Top: Oscar Brand
    Bottom: Barbara Dane, photo by Zoe Lowenthal
P. 18 Brownie McGhee
P. 19 Sam Hinton, photo by Mike and Lucy Parker
P. 21 Jack Elliott, photo by David Gahr
P. 22 Bottom: From "Music from the South" (Folkways Records), by Frederic Ramsey Jr.
    Top: The Tarriers, photo by David Gahr
P. 23 Big Bill Broonzy, photo by David Gahr
P. 27 Top: Woodcut
    Bottom: Illustration by Ben Shahn
P. 29 Harlequin with Guitar, by Juan Gris (1919)
P. 30 The New Lost City Ramblers, photo by David Gahr
P. 31 Top: Bob Dylan, photo by David Gahr
    Bottom: Jerry Silverman, photo by Don Weinapple
P. 32 Pablo Picasso
P. 33 Photo by Frederic Ramsey Jr.
P. 34 Woodrow Wilson Guthrie, photo by Sid Grossman
P. 35 Bud and Travis, photo by W. Field
P. 36 Pen and Ink Drawing by Peter Gordon (from SING OUT magazine)
P. 37 Joan Baez, photo by P. Wensberg
P. 39 Guy Carawan, photo by David Gahr
P. 40 Top: Woman with a Guitar, by Pablo Picasso (1909)
    Bottom: Cisco Houston
P. 41 Top: Pen and Ink Illustration by Dina Suller
    Bottom: The Carter Family, from Folkways Records "Anthology of American Folk Music" (Harry Smith)
P. 42 Frank Hamilton, photo by David Gahr
P. 43 Still Life: Guitar and Grapes, by Pablo Picasso
P. 45 Bill McAdoo, photo by David Gahr
P. 46 Top: Charlotte Anthony, photo by Sid Grossman
    Bottom: Richard Dyer-Bennet, photo by Sid Grossman
P. 47 Snooks Eaglin, courtesy Dr. Harry Oster
P. 48 Old Man with Guitar, by Pablo Picasso (Blue Period)
P. 49 Top: Bluegrass Group, photo by John Cohen
    Center: (Left to Right) Doc Watson, Clarence Ashley, Gaither Carlton
    Bottom: Earl Scruggs and Lester Flatt, photo by W. Field
    Bottom Left: Mandolin and Guitar, Pablo Picasso (1924)
P. 50 The Clancy Brothers and Tommy Makem, photo by David Gahr
P. 51 Top: The Brothers Four, photo by P. Wensberg
    Bottom: At The Newport Folk Festival, photo by W. Field
P. 52 Top: Lightning Hopkins, photo by David Gahr
    Bottom: Hogman Maxey (Folk-Lyric Records)
P. 53 Top: Czech Guitar Battente
    Bottom: Guitar made by Viennese Lute Maker, Matthias Fux
P. 55 Odetta, photo by P. Wensberg
P. 57 Ed Badeaux, photo by Mary Badeaux
P. 59 Earl Scruggs and Lester Flatt, photo by David Gahr
P. 61 Guitar, by Pablo Picasso (Crystal Period, 1916)
P. 62 Top: "The Harlem Hepcats"
    Bottom: Guitar Class, Folk Music Workshop, Idyllwild Arts Foundation, California, photo by Paul Pospesil
P. 63 Woman and Guitar, Braque (1913)
P. 65 Top: The Lord Invader (with rattles) and Calypso Group, photo by Sid Grossman
    Bottom: The Diaz Sisters, Chilean Folksingers (Folkways Records)
P. 66 The Gospel Keys
P. 68 Folksingers in Washington Square, NYC
P. 69 Beginners Guitar Group at Lincoln Farm Work Camp
P. 73 Original Woodcut, Cover Sheet Music Folio, by Posada
P. 74 Viennese Guitar
P. 75 Italian Guitars of the 17th and 18th Century

INDEX OF SONGS